Be My Guest

English for the Hotel Industry

Student's Book

Francis O'Hara

CAMBRIDGE
UNIVERSITY PRESS

CAMBRIDGE UNIVERSITY PRESS
Cambridge, New York, Melbourne, Madrid, Cape Town, Singapore, São Paulo, Delhi

Cambridge University Press
The Edinburgh Building, Cambridge CB2 8RU, UK

www.cambridge.org
Information on this title: www.cambridge.org/9780521776899

First published 2002
8th printing 2008

Printed in Dubai by Oriental Press

A catalogue record for this publication is available from the British Library

ISBN 978-0-521-77689-9 Student's Book
ISBN 978-0-521-77688-2 Teacher's Book
ISBN 978-0-521-77686-8 Audio CD Set
ISBN 978-0-521-77687-5 Audio Cassette Set

Contents

Thanks & acknowledgements

A very special 'thank you' to all my students over the years who have been teaching me what to write in *Be My Guest*.

To Beatriz de Orleans Borbón, for her constant generosity, encouragement and enriching insight on innumerable occasions.

To Will Capel who commissioned the project and whose skilful and patient handling of it has been invaluable.

To Vincent Olive in Monaco for his kindness in supplying very valuable information on hotels around the world.

To the Director, Jean Orselli, the teachers, and all my students at Audra Langues, Nice, France, who gave me the opportunity to develop the material in *Be My Guest*.

To Alison Silver for her enthusiastic and expert editing of *Be My Guest*, without whom many of my errors might have gone uncorrected.

To the Directors and staff of the following hotels who have generously allowed me to use authentic material from their publications.

    Le Meridien Shelbourne Hotel, Dublin, Ireland

    Hotel Royal Savoy, Lausanne, Switzerland

    Hotel Como, Melbourne, Australia

    Hotel Grande Bretagne, Athens, Greece

    Okura Garden Hotel, Shanghai, China

    Hotel Plaza, Nice, France

    Old Ship Hotel, Brighton, UK

    Princess Sofia Intercontinental Hotel,
      Barcelona, Spain

    Keio Plaza Hotel, Tokyo, Japan

    Carlton Hotel, New York, USA

Thanks also to Sally Smith for picture research, and Ruth Carim for proof-reading.

Recordings produced by James Richardson at Studio AVP, London.

Design and page make-up by Pentacor Book Design, High Wycombe.

Cover design by Dale Tomlinson.

The author and the publisher would like to thank the following for permission to reproduce photographs and other illustrative material:

Page 8 (top) and photos 1–5 Le Meridien Shelbourne Hotel, Dublin; page 8 photos 6 and 8 Getty Images (FPG); page 8 photo 7 Corbis UK Ltd; page 8 photo 9 Art Directors and TRIP Photo Library/N.Kealey, with thanks to Hotel East 21, Tokyo; page 8 photo 10 Pictor International; pages 19 and 34 www.CartoonStock.com; page 24 Hotel Royal Savoy, Lausanne; page 24 Hotel Como, Melbourne, Australia; page 26 Grande Bretagne Hotel, Athens, Greece; page 26 Okura Garden Hotel, Shanghai, China; page 30 Hotel Plaza, Nice, France; page 32 (photo and menu) Old Ship Hotel, Brighton, UK; page 34 Princess Sofia Intercontinental Hotel, Barcelona, Spain; page 40 (bar photos) Keio Plaza Hotel, Tokyo, Japan; page 52 Robert Harding Picture Library/Nigel Francis; page 53 Carlton Hotel, New York, USA.

Commissioned photographs by Gareth Boden on pages 12, 14, 39, 40 (left), 60 and 64.

A special thank you to the staff at The Manor of Groves Hotel, Hertfordshire and Down Hall Hotel, Hertfordshire for their help.

Art direction and picture research by Sally Smith.

Illustrations by Kate Charlesworth, Paul Cox c/o Arena, Neil Gower, Mark McLaughlin, Lee Montgomery, Peters and Zabransky.

Introduction

Welcome to *Be My Guest*

If you are already working, or intend to work, in the hotel industry and you use English in your work, then *Be My Guest* will help you to understand, speak, read and write the English you need.

The course is for students at the elementary and lower-intermediate levels. Its primary aim is to teach you to speak to and understand guests at the hotel where you work, in order to make their stay more comfortable and your job more enjoyable.

There are 15 units in the Student's Book, each based on a different work situation, including:

- Reception work
- Restaurant and bar work
- Answering the phone and taking messages
- Writing short e-mails and letters
- Dealing with guests' problems
- Explaining how things work
- Giving directions inside and outside the hotel
- Suggesting places to visit in the region

Each unit has two main parts. Part A introduces the topic and Part B develops it. In each part there are five sections to help you practise speaking, listening, reading and writing, as follows:

Presentation – this sets the scene and introduces a topic such as speaking on the phone, or suggesting places to visit in the region, etc.

Listening and pronunciation – this teaches you to understand guests (and hotel employees) as they make reservations, or explain a problem in the hotel, etc.

Language focus and practice – this practises the main language points of the unit, and is directly linked to the presentation and listening exercises.

Personal job file – here you personalise your work by applying what you have learnt in each lesson to your own specific situation at work. There are tips and exercises to help you remember what you have learnt, and you write down and translate the language items from the lesson that you need in your work in the hotel.

Speaking practice – here you bring all the work from the lesson together and you speak in pairs or small groups. You use the language you heard in the Listening section and do different exercises to practise what you have learnt.

Above all, have some fun while you are learning English.

Good luck!

Francis O'Hara

Map of the book

Unit	Page	Listening and pronunciation	Language focus and practice	Personal job file	Speaking practice
1 Introductions	8	Alphabet; spelling names; word stress	Verb *to be*; 'What's his/her/your name/job?', 'Where are you from?' etc.; countries, nationalities	Questions and answers: names, jobs and countries	Introductions: names, spelling, jobs, countries, nationalities
2 The check-in	12	Room bookings by e-mail; confirmation letters	Days, months, dates; language of confirmation letters	Confirmation letter; check-in dialogue	Dealing with changes in bookings; checking in
3 The hotel bedroom	16	Bedroom objects in standard and luxury rooms	'There is/are' in questions, affirmatives, negatives; *all, most, some, none*	Describing a standard and luxury hotel bedroom	Describing differences in hotel bedrooms; designing a hotel bedroom
4 Bathroom & porter	20	Range of bathroom objects; porter taking guests to their room	Prepositions of place; describing luggage colour, size, shape; polite offers and questions	Describing a hotel bathroom; dialogue between porter and guests	Designing a hotel bathroom; dialogue between porter and guests
5 Services in the hotel	24	Vocabulary of hotel services; opening and closing times of services	Time; *can, have, do, does* in questions, affirmatives, negatives	Questions and answers: services in the hotel	Giving opening and closing times of hotel services; discussion about most important services
6 Location of facilities	28	Understanding requests for directions; giving directions inside and outside the hotel	*To be, can, look*; verbs of direction, *turn left/right*, etc.; prepositions of place	Giving directions inside and outside the hotel	Explaining where services are; giving directions in and near the hotel
7 Room services	32	Taking room service orders; understanding availability and non-availability of different services	Checking food orders; apologising and giving reasons; past tense	Dealing with room services in the hotel	Taking, checking and correcting room service orders; explaining availability and non-availability of services
8 Problems & solutions	36	Understanding guests' problems during their stay; understanding how things work	Future, *I'll contact / send up*, etc.; verbs, *turn on/off, open, close*, etc.	Dealing with problems and solutions in the hotel; writing instructions	Understanding guests' problems during their stay and offering solutions

Unit	Page	Listening and pronunciation	Language focus and practice	Personal job file	Speaking practice
9 Taking bar orders	40	Taking orders for drinks; dealing with payment	Welcoming; offering choices of drinks; serving drinks; the bill, payment, tip	Building conversations in the hotel bar	Taking bar orders; dealing with different types of payment
10 In the restaurant (1)	44	Welcoming guests; taking orders for the starter, main course, and drinks	Greeting and seating guests; aperitifs; taking orders and explaining dishes for the starter, main course, and drinks	Describing and recommending dishes in the restaurant	Taking orders; recommending and explaining dishes; recommending specific wines
11 In the restaurant (2)	48	Dealing with orders for desserts, cheeses, and coffee; correcting mistakes on the bill	First conditional; recommending; asking about the meal; the bill	Describing popular desserts in the restaurant; dialogue about the meal	Describing desserts; taking orders; suggesting dishes; describing items on the menu; dealing with the bill
12 Places to visit	52	Understanding requests for places to visit; brochure article about Rome	Verbs, including modals, for recommending places to visit; comparatives and superlatives	Describing and recommending places to visit in the region	Making suggestions about places to visit; describing tourist sights
13 Enquiries	56	Understanding information on room rates; room types; conference equipment; numbers; currencies	Writing letters about room rates, and conference facilities; answering enquiries; offering help	Answering enquiry letters about rooms and conference facilities	Exchange of information on room rates, and conference facilities; choosing essential items for conferences
14 Using the phone	60	Responding to phone bookings; taking different types of phone messages	Dealing with booking problems, apologising, offering alternatives; telephone language: verbs and phrases	Beginning and ending phone conversations; taking a booking; taking phone messages	Dealing with phone bookings and problems, apologising, and offering alternatives; dealing with phone messages
15 The check-out	64	Understanding hotel bills in general, and specific items on the bill; numbers	Present perfect and past simple – affirmatives, questions, negatives	Questions and answers: the hotel bill; saying goodbye to guests	Presenting the hotel bill, methods of payment, and explaining specific items; tipping; saying goodbye

1 Introductions

Part A *Hello, I'm Zita, I'm a receptionist.*

1.1 PRESENTATION

Look at the photos of staff at Le Meridien Shelbourne Hotel, Dublin, Ireland.

Study the job titles and then match each photo with a job.

Le Meridien Shelbourne Hotel, Dublin, Ireland

1

Zita

2

Akoun

3

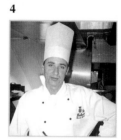

Jimmy

4

Shaun

5

Niamh

A I'm a commissionaire.
D I'm a sous-chef.

B I'm a receptionist.
E I'm a kitchen assistant.

C I'm a waitress.

Here are some more employees from different hotels around the world.

What do you think they do? Match each photo with a job.

6

My name's Taki.

7

I'm Teresa.

8

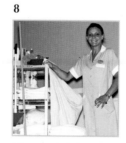

My name's Anita.

9

I'm Yoshida.

10

I'm Kelly.

F I'm a bar person.
I I'm a management trainee.

G I'm a porter.
J I'm a waiter.

H I'm a chambermaid / room attendant.

Is YOUR job here? What do you do? What's your job?

1.2 LISTENING AND PRONUNCIATION

1 Now check your answers. Listen to the ten employees in 1.1 saying who they are.
Notice the short sound /ə/ in 'I'm <u>a</u> waitress.'
Notice the word stress, e.g. re'ceptionist, 'waitress.

2 Here is the alphabet. Listen and repeat it.

A B C D E F G H I J K L M N O P Q R S T U V W X Y Z

3 You will hear ten names. Listen to the way the names are spelt and repeat them.

1.3 LANGUAGE FOCUS AND PRACTICE

Questions and answers
Study the following questions and answers.

Question	Answer
What's your name?	I'm Anita. / My name's Anita.
What's your job? ⎫	I'm a chambermaid.
What do you do? ⎭	I'm a chambermaid.
What's his name?	His name's Jimmy.
What's her name?	Her name's Niamh.
What's his job?	He's a commissionaire.
What's her job?	She's a waitress.

Now write the question.

1 _____? Her name's Kelly.

2 _____? She's a waitress.

3 _____? My name's Taki.

4 _____? His name's Shaun.

5 _____? I'm a waiter.

6 _____? He's a commissionaire.

1.4 PERSONAL JOB FILE

Go to your **Job file** on page 69. Write down any new words and phrases.
Complete the questions and answers.

1.5 SPEAKING PRACTICE *In groups*

1 Introduce yourself. Learn the name of each person in your group, and how to spell it.
Study this question.

Question: Could you spell that, please?
Answer: Yes, of course, it's S-H-A-U-N.

2 Find out the job of each person in your group. Notice how we use 'yes' and 'no'.

Question: Are you a waiter?
Answer: Yes, I am. / No, I'm a porter.

3 Introduce your group to the class.

Part B *Where are you from?*

They're from Ireland.

We're from Italy.

She's from the USA.

He's from Japan.

I'm from Greece.

1.6 PRESENTATION

Where are you from?
Mark your country on the map.
Now ask your partner like this:

Question: Where are you from?
Answer: I'm from Dublin, Ireland.

These are the five employees
from the Shelbourne Hotel.
Where do you think they are from?

Niamh	Shaun	Zita	Akoun	Jimmy
Australia	Ireland	Ireland	Ireland	France

These are the other five employees from around the world. Where do you think they are from?

Taki	Teresa	Anita	Yoshida	Kelly
USA	England	Japan	Italy	Greece

1.7 LISTENING AND PRONUNCIATION

You will hear the ten employees introducing themselves. Listen and check your answers.

1.8 LANGUAGE FOCUS AND PRACTICE

1 To be Complete the table.

Affirmative	Negative	Question
I'm	I'm not	Am I?
--------------------	--------------------	Are you?
He's / She's / It's	--------------------	Is he? Is she? Is it?
--------------------	We're not	--------------------
You're	--------------------	--------------------
--------------------	They're not	Are they?

2 Study these sentences.

Question: Are you American?   *Answers:* Yes, I am. / No, I'm not, I'm Australian.
Question: Where are they from?   *Answers:* They're from Ireland.   They're Irish.

Complete the sentences about yourself.

I'm from _____   I'm _____

Now ask your partner.

Complete the gaps.

She's from _____   She's _____
He's from _____   He's _____

10

3 Study this extract from the conversation in 1.7.

NIAMH : Hello, my name's Niamh, I'm from Ireland.

AKOUN : Nice to meet you, Niamh. I'm Akoun.

NIAMH : Where are you from, Akoun?

AKOUN : I'm from France.

NIAMH : Oh really, which part?

AKOUN : The south, near Nice.

4 Put the words in these sentences in the correct order.

1

A I'm Hello Anita I'm Italy from

B part Hey too me which

A The Naples south

B I'm from Oh Rome

2

A she's Hello is Zita Kelly American this

B Kelly from Hi what are of part America you

A west The California

3

A meet Akoun Hello to nice you

B too You

1.9 PERSONAL JOB FILE

Go to your Job file on page 69. Write down any new words and phrases.
Complete the 'introductions' dialogue.

1.10 SPEAKING PRACTICE *In groups*

1 Go to page 97 and study Tapescript 1.7.
Practise the conversations first with the tapescript, then without. Change roles.

2 Introduce yourself and then introduce a partner to the group.
Then introduce yourself and your group to the whole class.

2 The check-in

Part A *I have a reservation.*

2.1 PRESENTATION

1 Is this like the reception area of the hotel you work in? How different is it?

2 Look at these room types. Match each to an abbreviation.

S2   S2D   DA   S   FD   D

single room   double room – one bed
twin room   double room – twin beds
one-bed suite   de-luxe double

2.2 LISTENING AND PRONUNCIATION

1 Read Mr Bouvier's e-mail. Is there a room available for him? Complete the reservations chart.

Dear Sir or Madam,

I'd like to reserve a double room with bath, from 18–21 July, if possible with a balcony.

Yours sincerely,

Jacques Bouvier

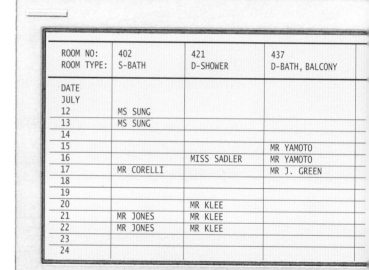

ROOM NO: ROOM TYPE:	402 S-BATH	421 D-SHOWER	437 D-BATH, BALCONY
DATE JULY			
12	MS SUNG		
13	MS SUNG		
14			
15			MR YAMOTO
16		MISS SADLER	MR YAMOTO
17	MR CORELLI		MR J. GREEN
18			
19			
20		MR KLEE	
21	MR JONES	MR KLEE	
22	MR JONES	MR KLEE	
23			
24			

2 Now listen to Mr Bouvier. He wants to change his reservation. Is there a suitable room available? Make changes to the chart.

3 Look at these days and dates, then listen and repeat them.

	JANUARY				
M	1	8	15	22	29
T	2	9	16	23	30
W	3	10	17	24	31
T	4	11	18	25	
F	5	12	19	26	
S	6	13	20	27	
S	7	14	21	28	

Monday   Tuesday   Wednesday   Thursday   Friday
Saturday   Sunday

1st January   2nd February   3rd March   4th April
5th May   6th June   7th July   8th August
9th September   10th October   11th November
12th December

first   twenty-first   thirty-first   second   twenty-second
third   twenty-third   fourth   twenty-fourth

4 Listen to these questions and answer them. Then ask a partner.

1 What's today's date?
2 What's your day off?
3 When is the next national holiday?

4 When do you go on holiday?
5 When's your birthday?

2.3 LANGUAGE FOCUS AND PRACTICE

1 Reading and writing

In **2.2** you heard Mr Bouvier change his reservation. This is the confirmation reply sent by the hotel.

Dear Mr Bouvier,

Further to our earlier telephone conversation, we are pleased to confirm your new booking as follows:

Arrival:	19 July	*Departure:*	22 July
Room type:	Double room with bath and balcony		
Room rate:	$189		
Confirmation:	JU19 FD1 408		

We look forward to welcoming you on 19 July.

Yours sincerely,

2 Another guest, Ms Sung, wants to change her reservation.

Here is part of the e-mail she sent. What change does she want to make?

Dear Sir or Madam,

I have a reservation for two nights, the 12th and 13th July for a single room with bath. I would like to change the dates, if possible, to the 15th and 16th July ...

Check the reservations chart. Is it possible?

Now write the reply. Put these phrases into the correct order to complete the letter of confirmation to Ms Sung.

_1_ Dear Ms Sung,

..... Thank you for your e-mail of ...

..... your new reservation as follows:

..... We are pleased to confirm

..... to welcoming you on the 15th July.

..... Confirmation: JU15 S2B 393

..... Arrival: 15th July   Departure: 17th July

..... Room rate: €99 per night

..... We look forward

..... Room type: single room with bath

..... Kind regards,

2.4 PERSONAL JOB FILE

Go to your Job file on page 70. Write down any new words and phrases. Write in the dates. Complete the confirmation letter.

2.5 SPEAKING PRACTICE *In pairs*

Student A: You are the receptionist. Go to page 97 and study Tapescript **2.2**.
Student B: You are the guest. Go to page 97 and study Tapescript **2.2**.

Practise the conversation first with the tapescript, then without. Change roles.

Part B *Here's your key sir, it's on the fourth floor, room 401.*

2.6 PRESENTATION

1

When guests arrive at reception, what do you say to them?

Study these sentences. Which are polite and which are not polite? Say why. Write P or NP.

...... Hello, can I help you?

...... Do you have a reservation?

...... Hello, what do you want?

...... And your name, please?

...... I'm sorry, the hotel is full.

...... We have nothing for you.

2 Mr and Mrs Bouvier arrive at reception. First mark the sentences G(uest) or R(eceptionist). Then put the sentences in order to make the dialogue between the guest and the receptionist. Two have been done for you.

_R_ _1_ Good evening sir, good evening madam.

.... Thank you. Bouvier, yes, ... so that's a double room with bath and balcony for three nights.

.... Thank you sir, here's your key. It's on the fourth floor, room 401.

.... Yes, of course.

.... Could you just sign here, please?

.... B-O-U-V-I-E-R.

.... Could you spell that, please?

.... Thank you.

.... Good evening, we have a reservation, the name's Bouvier.

...... _6_ That's right.

.... I'll call a porter.

.... Enjoy your stay.

2.7 LISTENING AND PRONUNCIATION

1 Listen to the conversation above and check your answers.

2

Being clear and polite Listen to these sentences and repeat them.	
Good evening sir, good evening madam.	Could you sign here, please?
Could you spell that, please?	Here's your key.
That's a double room with bath and balcony for three nights.	It's room 401, on the fourth floor.
	I'll call a porter.

2.8   LANGUAGE FOCUS AND PRACTICE

Checking in

This conversation is like the one you heard in 2.7.
Complete it using these words.

seventh floor   spell   sign here   a reservation   six nights
Thank you   here's your   single room   your name   call him
Good evening   right   Would you like   Good evening

RECEPTIONIST	........................, madam.
GUEST	.... I have ....
RECEPTIONIST	And ...., madam?
GUEST	Wolfington.
RECEPTIONIST	Could you .... that, please?
GUEST	W-O-L-F-I-N-G-T-O-N.
RECEPTIONIST	........................, Mrs Wolfington, yes, a .... and shower for ....
GUEST	That's ....
RECEPTIONIST	Could you just ...., please?
GUEST	Yes, of course.
RECEPTIONIST	Thank you, madam, ... key. It's room 738 on the ....
RECEPTIONIST	.... a porter?
GUEST	Yes, please.
RECEPTIONIST	I'll just .... Enjoy your stay.
GUEST	Thank you.

2.9   PERSONAL JOB FILE

Go to your Job file on page 70. Write down any new words and phrases.
A guest is checking in. Complete the dialogue using your own words.

2.10   SPEAKING PRACTICE *In pairs*

1

Student A: You are the guest. Go to pages 97–98 and study Tapescript 2.7.
Student B: You are the receptionist. Go to pages 97–98 and study Tapescript 2.7.

Practise the conversation first with the tapescript and then without. Change roles.

2

Students A and B: In the same way, practise the dialogue you completed in 2.8.

Change roles.

3 The hotel bedroom

FOCUS: DESCRIBING STANDARD AND LUXURY HOTEL ROOMS

Part A *Can you describe the room, please?*

3.1 PRESENTATION

Look at these objects.

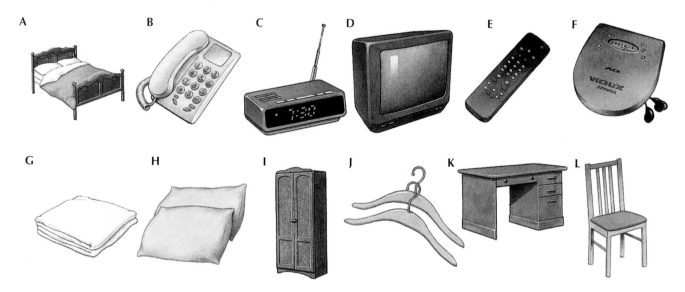

Look at this list of objects and label the illustrations.

double bed   sheets   chair   radio alarm   CD player   TV
coat hangers   pillows   telephone   wardrobe   desk   remote control

3.2 LISTENING AND PRONUNCIATION

1 A guest is enquiring about a room. Listen to the hotel employee and number the objects in the order you hear them. The first has been done for you.

1 double bed   ...... CD player   ...... desk   ...... remote control

...... TV   ...... coat hangers   ...... chair   ...... pillows

...... sheets   ...... wardrobe   ...... radio alarm   ...... telephone

2

Being clear and polite   Listen to these sentences and repeat them.

There's a telephone by the bed.

You have the radio alarm next to that.

The sheets are changed every day.

There's a TV of course, with remote control.

I'm afraid there isn't a CD player in the room, madam.

There are plenty of coat hangers.

There's a desk by the window, with two very comfortable chairs.

3.3 LANGUAGE FOCUS AND PRACTICE

There is / There are

Study these structures:

Singular	Plural
There is a mini-bar in every room.	There are plenty of coat hangers.
There isn't a CD player in the room.	There aren't any plants in the room.
Is there a TV in every room?	Are there any flowers in the room?

Put the words in the following sentences in the correct order. The first has been done for you.

Singular

Affirmative: is   TV   in   room   There   a   the

Example: *There is a TV in the room.* ....

Negative: double bed   isn't   There   a   in   room   the

....

Question: CD player   there   room   in   Is   a   the   ?

....

Answers: is   there   Yes   /   the   room   Yes   there   CD player   in   a   is

....   /   ....

there   isn't   No   /   CD player   No   there   in   room   isn't   a   the

....   /   ....

Plural

Affirmative: coat hangers   of   plenty   wardrobe   There   are   the   in

....

Negative: in   room   There   aren't   the   flowers   any

....

Question: the   plants   there   in   Are   any   room   ?

....

Answers: are   Yes   there   /   room   some   in   plants   Yes   there   the   are

....   /   ....

there   No   aren't   /   any   there   room   plants   No   aren't   the   in

....   /   ....

3.4 PERSONAL JOB FILE

Go to your Job file on page 71. Write down any new words and phrases.
Describe a standard bedroom in the hotel where you work.

3.5 SPEAKING PRACTICE   *In pairs*

Game: Spot the difference

Student A: Go to page 84 and study the drawing in Speaking practice **3.5A**.
Student B: Go to page 92 and study the drawing in Speaking practice **3.5B**.

Ask questions to discover the differences between the rooms in the drawings.
List the differences. When you have finished, write them down and tell the class.

Part B *There's full air-conditioning, of course.*

3.6 PRESENTATION

What items would you expect to find in a luxury hotel bedroom?

Look at these three hotel bedrooms. Which is most like a bedroom in the hotel where you work?

air-conditioning

Bedroom A

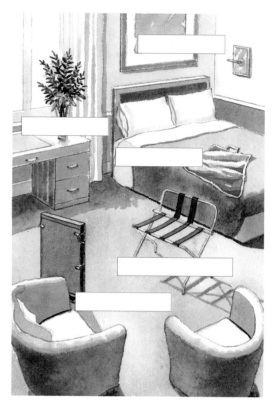

Bedroom B

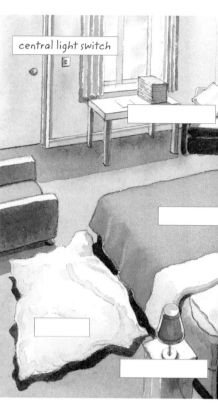

central light switch

Bedroom C

Look at this list of words:

mini-bar   blanket   duvet   bedside lamp   suitcase stand   desk   central light switch
trouser press   laundry bag   air-conditioning   writing paper   flowers   plant   personal safe

Label the objects in the three illustrations. Two have already been labelled.

3.7 LISTENING AND PRONUNCIATION

1 Listen to four conversations where guests are enquiring about rooms. The hotel employee describes each of the four rooms. Listen and identify the three hotel rooms above.

2

Being clear and polite   Listen to these sentences and repeat them.

We can give you a very quiet room on the top floor.

Everything you need is included in the room.

It's small but very quiet.

I'm afraid there isn't a mini-bar in the room.

It's a large sunny room with a view of the sea.

There's full air-conditioning, of course.

3.8 LANGUAGE FOCUS AND PRACTICE

Describing rooms

In 3.7 you heard these words used in the descriptions of the rooms:

All of the rooms …	= 100%
Most of the rooms …	= over 50%
Some of the rooms …	= under 50%
None of the rooms …	= 0%

Study this description and complete the sentences below with one of these phrases.

Hotel RITA

- ◆ 33 rooms + 3 suites, all with full air-conditioning

- ◆ 3 suites: four-poster bed, en-suite luxury bathroom, TV

- ◆ 17 double rooms: king-size bed, en-suite bathroom, TV

- ◆ 10 double rooms: twin beds, en-suite bathroom, TV

- ◆ 6 single rooms: shower only, WC

- ◆ Personal safe available at reception

- ◆ Fax machines and computers with internet access available in the conference room only

In the Hotel Rita:

1 .... air-conditioning.
2 .... a personal safe.
3 .... twin beds.
4 .... a TV.
5 .... a four-poster bed.
6 .... a fax machine.
7 .... a shower and WC only.
8 .... a king-size bed.
9 .... a luxury bathroom.
10 .... a computer.

3.9 PERSONAL JOB FILE

Go to your Job file on page 71. Write down any new words and phrases. Describe a luxury bedroom in the hotel where you work.

3.10 SPEAKING PRACTICE *In groups*

Design your own hotel room

Go to page 85 where you will see a basic plan of a hotel bedroom. Design your ideal hotel room. When you have finished, describe it to the class.

4 Bathroom & porter

Part A *Can you send up some more towels, please?*

4.1   PRESENTATION

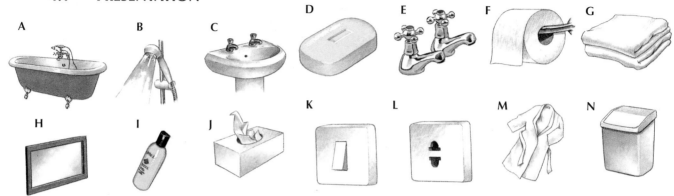

1 Look at these objects.

Look at this list of objects and label the pictures.

shampoo   bin   shower   mirror   washbasin   toilet paper   towels   bath   bathrobe
tissues   light switch   soap   hot/cold water taps   shaver socket

2 Read these sentences. Who would say them? Write R→G or G→R or H→M next to each sentence. The first one has been done for you.

R→G = Receptionist to Guest   G→R = Guest to Receptionist   H→M = Housekeeper to Maid

1 Yes, madam, all the doubles have a bath. R→G
2 Can you send up some more towels, please?
3 Some of the single rooms have a shower only.
4 There's a light switch next to the mirror, sir.
5 Yes, sir, there's always plenty of hot water.
6 Could we have some more shampoo and soap, please?
7 Make sure there's always plenty of toilet paper.
8 We keep the extra tissues in the cupboard under the washbasin.
9 There should be a bathrobe just behind the door, madam.
10 Don't forget to empty the bin every time.

4.2   LISTENING AND PRONUNCIATION

1 Look at this illustration of a bathroom.

2   Complete these sentences using the following words.

mirror   tap   extra tissues   shaver socket   bathrobe   bin   shower   soap   washbasin   towels

1   We keep .... and toilet paper here in the cupboard.

2   The .... is on the wall next to the ....

3   The .... is here under the ....

4   There's a hot and cold mixer .... for the ....

5   The .... is here behind the door and the .... are on the rack over the bath.

6   Always put plenty of .... and shampoo here, near the taps.

3   Listen to a description of the bathroom and check your answers.
Now match sentences 1–6 to letters A–F in the illustration.

> **Being clear and polite**   **4**   Listen to the sentences and repeat them.

4.3   LANGUAGE FOCUS AND PRACTICE

1   Prepositions
Look at these prepositions. You heard them in 4.2.

next to   near   under   behind   over   in   on

2   <u>Underline</u> these prepositions in the sentences you completed in 4.2.

3   Look at this illustration.
Correct the prepositions in these sentences *only* if they are wrong.

1   A small hand towel is on the floor near the washbasin.
2   A box of tissues is behind the taps in the washbasin.
3   A large cupboard is over the washbasin.
4   The bathrobe is next to the bath.
5   The bin is behind the door near the bath.
6   The light switch is over the wall under the door.

4.4   PERSONAL JOB FILE

Go to your Job file on page 72. Write down any new words and phrases.
Describe a bathroom in the hotel where you work.

4.5   SPEAKING PRACTICE   *In groups*

Design your own hotel bathroom
Go to page 86 and look at the plan of a hotel bathroom. Design your ideal hotel bathroom using the words in this lesson. When you have finished, describe it to the class.

Part B *Can I help you with your luggage, madam?*

4.6 PRESENTATION

1 What do you think is being said in the picture? Is this like a scene at the hotel where you work? What's the same? What's different?

2 The porter is taking the guest's luggage to the room. Put the sentences in the correct order to make a conversation between the porter and the guest. The first and last have been done for you.

PORTER	*1*	Can I help you with your luggage, madam?
GUEST	......	Thank you, and here's something for you.
GUEST	......	Yes, please, those two red suitcases are mine.
PORTER	......	This way, please, madam, the lift is just over there.

PORTER	......	Shall I take the small green bag too?
GUEST	......	Oh yes, please bring it as well.
PORTER	......	Here you are, madam, room 233.
PORTER	*8*	Thank you very much, madam, I hope you enjoy your stay.

4.7 LISTENING AND PRONUNCIATION

1 Listen to the conversation in **4.6** and check your answers.

2 Study these five sentences.

1 Can I help you with your luggage, madam?
2 Shall I take the small green bag too?
3 This way, please, the lift is just over there.

4 Here you are, madam, room 233.
5 Thank you very much, madam, I hope you enjoy your stay.

Look at these five pictures and match each one with a sentence.

A   B   C   D   E

3

Being clear and polite   Listen to these sentences and repeat them.
Can I help you with your luggage, madam?   Here you are, madam, room 233.
Shall I take the small green bag too?   Thank you very much, madam, I hope you
This way, please, madam, the lift is just   enjoy your stay.
over there.

4.8 LANGUAGE FOCUS AND PRACTICE

1 Adjectives and colours

Do you know these words? Label each colour.

red green yellow brown orange
black blue white pink grey beige

What is your favourite colour?
What colour is the room you are in?

2 Look at these adjectives:

square big light nylon old round heavy new leather small

3 Choose a colour and an adjective to describe each item of luggage, like this: 'a small red case'.

A   B   C   D   E

F   G   H   I   J

4 Polite offers and questions

A polite offer: Shall I take the small green bag too?   Shall I + *infinitive*
A polite question: Would you like a porter?   Would you like ...?

Put the words in the right order in these sentences.

1 take Shall case small I the red

   ---------------------------------?

2 I bring all bags these Shall

   ---------------------------------?

3 too you this Would orange like big bag

   ---------------------------------?

4 madam boxes How these about

   ---------------------------------?

5 way madam This please

   ----

6 lift is The over just there

   ----

7 your 707 madam Here's room

   ----

8 I you your enjoy holiday hope

4.9 PERSONAL JOB FILE

Go to your Job file on page 72. Write down any new words and phrases.
Complete the three stages of the conversation between the guest and porter.

4.10 SPEAKING PRACTICE *In pairs*

Student A: You are the guest. Go to page 98 and study Tapescript **4.7**.
Student B: You are the porter. Go to page 98 and study Tapescript **4.7**.

Practise the conversation between the guest and the porter, first with the tapescript,
then without. Change roles.

5 Services in the hotel

FOCUS: FACILITIES IN THE HOTEL; OPENING AND CLOSING TIMES

Part A *What time does the restaurant open, please?*

5.1 PRESENTATION

Look at these services and label the pictures.

Bar   Restaurant   Fitness centre
Car park   Reception   Swimming pool
Room service   Laundry service

How many of these services are in the hotel where you work?

Look at the services in the hotels below. Look at the opening and closing times. What time do you think the services in the hotels open and close?

Service	Opening and closing times
Fitness & sauna	Open in summer
Restaurant	Available until 10.30 pm
Room service	Open every day from 7 am to 10 pm
Swimming pool	Open every evening until 10 pm

*Hotel Royal Savoy,
Lausanne, Switzerland*

The Hotel Como
Melbourne
• EXPECT THE VERY BEST •

Service	Opening and closing times
Bar	By 11 am
Laundry	24 hour valet service
Check-in	Opens at 4 pm
Check-out	Same day
Parking	From 2 pm

*Hotel Como,
Melbourne, Australia*

5.2 LISTENING AND PRONUNCIATION

 1 Listen to the conversations between the employees and guests at the Hotel Royal Savoy and the Hotel Como, about the services in the two hotels. Match the times and services in 5.1.

2
Being clear and polite   Listen to these sentences and repeat them.

It's open every evening from 7 to around 10 o'clock.	... but it opens up again tomorrow at 7 am.
	The pool is only open in summer.
The fitness and sauna closes at 10 pm ...	Room service is available until 10.30 pm.

5.3 LANGUAGE FOCUS AND PRACTICE

1 Time Complete the times.

.... o'clock   one ....   a quarter past .... thirty   .... forty-five   half past ....

ten past .... past .... twenty   ten ....   a .... to twelve   .... fifty-five

2 Study these structures.

What time does it open?	It opens at 7 am.	It's open 7 days a week.
What time does it close?	It closes at 10 pm.	It's open from Monday to Friday.
When does it open and close?	It's open from 7 am to 10 pm.	It's open in summer/winter.
Is it open every day?	Yes, it is. / No, it isn't, I'm afraid.	

3 Complete the questions using these words.

available   service open   does
What is   late   by   Is   open

1   What time .... the fitness centre close?

2   .... the latest check-out time, please?

3   Is the laundry ....?
    I need these things .... tonight.

4   Is room service ....? I know it's a bit ....

5   .... the car park locked at night?

6   When does the bar ....?

Complete the answers using these words.

latest   24 hour   fitness   same-day
available   service   opens   closes at

A   Yes, sir, room .... is .... until 10.30.

B   The .... check-out is at 11 am.

C   It .... at 4 pm.

D   Yes, sir, and there's .... valet parking service.

E   The .... and sauna .... 10 pm.

F   Yes, madam, there is a .... laundry service.

Now match the questions in 1–6 with an answer in A–F.

5.4 PERSONAL JOB FILE

Go to your Job file on page 73. Write down any new words and phrases. Correct the mistakes in each question and answer given. Write four questions and answers about opening and closing times of services at the hotel where you work.

5.5 SPEAKING PRACTICE *In pairs*

1 *Student A:* You are the guest.   *Student B:* You are the hotel employee.   Practise the questions and answers from **5.3** exercise 3, first with your books open, then closed. Change roles.

2 *Student A:* You are the guest. Go to page 87. Study the information in Speaking practice **5.5A**. Ask the employee complete questions.

Student B: You are the hotel employee. Go to page 93. Study the information in Speaking practice **5.5B**. Using this information, give complete answers to the guest's questions.

Change roles.

Part B *We have a fully equipped business centre and a fitness centre.*

5.6 PRESENTATION

Look at these services and label the illustrations.

Computer services   Translations   Fitness centre   Sauna
Secretarial services   Conference rooms   Exercise
equipment   Audio-visual equipment   Internet access
Indoor swimming pool   Tour guides   Beauty salon

Which ones did you see in Part A? Which are
business and which are leisure activities? How many
of these services are in the hotel where you work?

5.7 LISTENING AND PRONUNCIATION

  1

Listen to the conversations between the hotel
employees and guests about the services at the Hotel Grande Bretagne,
Athens and the Okura Garden Hotel, Shanghai. Tick (✓) the services you hear.

In total, only 10 services are mentioned. Which two services are *not* mentioned?

	Grande Bretagne	Okura Garden		Grande Bretagne	Okura Garden
Sauna	_____	_____	Beauty salon	_____	_____
Fitness centre	_____	_____	Audio-visual equipment	_____	_____
Conference rooms	_____	_____	Exercise equipment	_____	_____
Internet access	_____	_____	Tour guide	_____	_____
Computer services	_____	_____	Translations	_____	_____
Secretarial services	_____	_____	Indoor swimming pool	_____	_____

*Hotel Grande Bretagne,
Athens, Greece*

2

> ### Being clear and polite   Listen to these sentences and repeat them.
>
> We have a fully equipped business
> centre, with internet access.
>
> We have a full range of secretarial
> services.
>
> We have full translation services.
>
> Just let us know in advance and
> we can arrange everything.
>
> There's a fully equipped
> fitness club with an indoor
> swimming pool.
>
> You'll find all the exercise
> equipment you need.
>
> There's a wonderful sauna.

*Okura Garden Hotel,
Shanghai, China*

5.8 LANGUAGE FOCUS AND PRACTICE

1   *Can* and *Have* Study these questions and answers.

Have you got cable TV in the hotel?   Yes, we have. / No, we haven't.
Has the hotel got an indoor pool?   Yes, it has. / No, it hasn't.
Can I/we send e-mails from here?   Yes, you can. / No, you can't.
Can she get a hair appointment at once?   Yes, she can. / No, she can't.

2 Complete these sentences using the verbs 'can' or 'have'.

1 .... he got the key?   No, ...
2 .... you got a fax machine?   Yes, ...
3 .... she use the fitness centre now?   Yes, ...
4 .... you do it by tonight?   No, ...

3 Complete the following sentences using these words.

we use   you can   can arrange   Have you   got   has   not   have   Can   arrange

1 Has the hotel .... an express laundry service? Yes, madam, it ....

2 .... we use the business centre now? Yes, sir, ... It's open until 8 pm.

3 .... got everything? Yes, I think I ....

4 Can you .... secretarial services? Yes, we .... everything.

5 Can .... the sauna now? I'm afraid .... sir, the sauna is closed.

4   A hotel brochure

Read the extract from a hotel brochure. Complete it using these words.

internet   secretarial   translation service   computer   audio-visual   conference
exercise   sauna   tour guide   beauty   health and fitness   indoor pool

We have a fully equipped business centre, including .... rooms with all the latest .... equipment. Our range of hi-tech .... services includes full .... access. We can arrange a full .... service, plus a full .... in several languages.

Enjoy the wonderful panoramic views over the mountains, as you work out in our .... club, with all the latest .... equipment. Visit the .... salon, go for a ...., or go for a swim in the heated .... If you would like to go sightseeing we can arrange for a .... to show you the sights.

5.9   PERSONAL JOB FILE

Go to your Job file on page 73. Write down any new words and phrases. Write four questions and answers about business and leisure services in the hotel where you work.

5.10   SPEAKING PRACTICE *In pairs*

1 *Student A:* You are the guest.   *Student B:* You are the hotel employee.
Together practise the questions and answers you completed in 5.8 exercises 2 and 3, first with the books open, then closed. Change roles.

2 *In groups* What services do you think are important? You have seen several in this lesson. List the six services which you think are the most important for your ideal hotel. Tell the class and say why you think they are important.

6 Location of facilities

FOCUS: GIVING DIRECTIONS TO FACILITIES IN AND NEAR THE HOTEL

Part A *The travel desk is on the ground floor.*

6.1 PRESENTATION

Do you know what these directions mean? Work in groups and make a simple drawing of each one.

turn right   turn left   go up   go down
next to   opposite

6.2 LISTENING AND PRONUNCIATION

1 Look at the plan of the hotel. Some guests are asking for directions in the hotel. Listen to the conversations and write down the place each guest is looking for.

Guest 1 ....

Guest 2 ....

Guest 3 ....

Guest 4 ....

Guest 5 ....

2 Listen again and label these three places on the hotel plan.

bar   business centre   swimming pool

3

> **Being clear and polite**
> **Listen to these sentences and repeat them.**
>
> The gift shop is in the basement.
>
> When you go out of the lift, turn right.
>
> It's in the main lobby, opposite the reception desk.
>
> It's inside the restaurant on the ground floor.
>
> Go down to the ground floor.
>
> As you come out of the lift, it's on your left.
>
> Out of the lift, turn right, and it's next to the conference rooms.

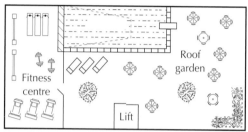

Top floor

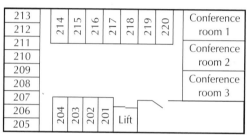

Second floor

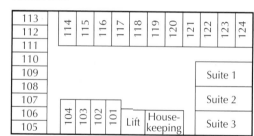

First floor

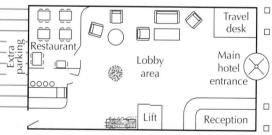

Ground floor

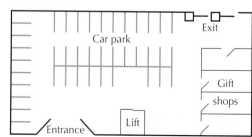

Basement

6.3 LANGUAGE FOCUS AND PRACTICE

1 **Three verbs** In **6.2**, the guests asked questions like this:

Be	Excuse me, where is the travel desk, please?
	Excuse me, the business centre is on the third floor, isn't it?
Can	Can you tell me where the gift shop is, please?
Look	I'm looking for the bar, please.

2 **Verbs of direction** The employee gives directions using these verbs:

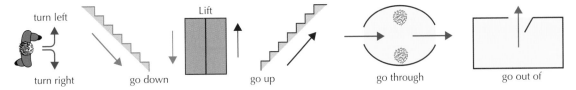

turn left / turn right   go down   Lift go up   go through   go out of

Look at the plan of the hotel. Complete these sentences.

1 To get to the gift shops, go out of the lift and ....

2 The restaurant is on the ground floor; .... the lobby and it's at the end.

3 To get to the business centre, ... to the second floor, and as you .... the lift it's on your right.

4 From your room, go .... to the restaurant near the lobby, and the bar is inside the restaurant.

5 The fitness centre is on the top floor; as you come out of the lift, ... and you'll see the fitness centre next to the pool.

3 **Prepositions of place** Look at the plan of the hotel. Complete the sentences below.

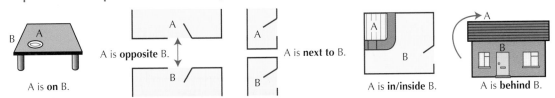

A is **on** B.   A is **opposite** B.   A is **next to** B.   A is **in/inside** B.   A is **behind** B.

1 The car park is .... the basement.

2 The travel desk is .... reception, in the lobby.

3 All the conference rooms are .... the second floor.

4 The pool is on the top floor, ... the fitness centre.

5 The bar is .... the restaurant.

6 You can also park just .... the hotel.

6.4 PERSONAL JOB FILE

Go to your Job file on page 74. Write down any new words and phrases. You are in the reception area of the hotel where you work. Choose four places guests want to go to inside the hotel. Start from reception. Write down these four directions for guests.

6.5 SPEAKING PRACTICE *In pairs*

Student A: You are the guest. Go to page 87 and study the plan of the hotel in Speaking practice **6.5A**. There are no services marked on it. Ask your partner where the services are and write their position on your plan.

Student B: You are the employee. Go to page 93 and study the plan of the hotel in Speaking practice **6.5B**. Tell your partner where the services are.

Check your answers. Change roles.

Part B *It's about a five-minute walk from here.*

6.6 PRESENTATION

Look at these names of places and label the illustrations.

Post office   Photo shop   Cash point
Shopping centre   Cinema   Bank
Travel agent   Railway station

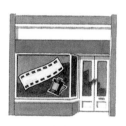

6.7 LISTENING AND PRONUNCIATION

1 Some guests are asking for directions to places outside the hotel. Listen to the conversations and write down the place each guest is looking for.

Guest 1 ....

Guest 2 ....

Guest 3 ....

Guest 4 ....

Guest 5 ....

2 You are at the Hotel Plaza in Nice. Look at the street plan. Listen and follow the directions you hear. Where does the guest want to go to?

The guest wants to go to ....

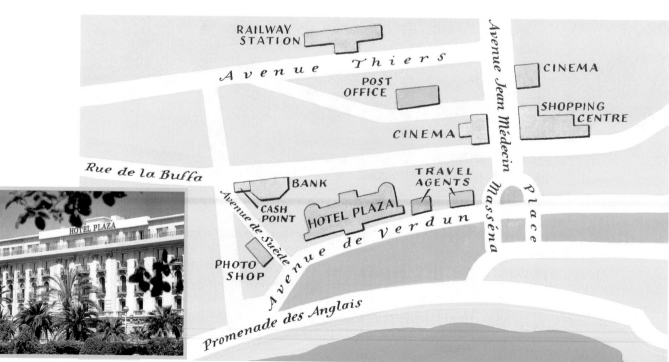

Hotel Plaza, Nice, France

🔊 **3**

> **Being clear and polite**   Listen to these sentences and repeat them.
>
> Certainly, it's not far.
>
> Go out of the hotel and turn left.
>
> Go along Avenue de Verdun for about 100 metres.
>
> It's just a few minutes walk.
>
> Go up Avenue de Suède until you get to Rue de la Buffa.
>
> The bank is on the corner, on your right.
>
> There's one very near the hotel in Avenue de Suède.
>
> It's about a 10-minute walk from here, sir.
>
> There on the corner, on your right, is the cash point next to the bank.

6.8   LANGUAGE FOCUS AND PRACTICE

1   **Directions**   Study these directions. You heard them in **6.7** exercise 1.

GUEST: I'm looking for a photo shop, please.

EMPLOYEE: There's one very near the hotel in Avenue de Suède. Go out of the hotel, turn right and go along to Avenue de Suède. Turn right into Avenue de Suède, and you'll see the photo shop opposite.

You are at the Hotel Plaza in Nice. Find the travel agents on the map. Complete the directions using these phrases.

turn left   go along   go out of   on your left   it's not far

GUEST: Good morning, can you help me? I'm looking for a travel agent, as I need to change my ticket.

EMPLOYEE: Certainly, ... from here. .... the hotel and .... and Avenue de Verdun for about 100 metres, and there are two travel agents ....

2   **You are at the Hotel Plaza. Find the shopping centre on the map and write out the directions using these phrases.**

turn left   out of the hotel   go along   until you get to   go up   on your right

To get to the shopping centre, go ....

....

3   Find an expression that is similar to 'It's not far'. ....

6.9   PERSONAL JOB FILE

Go to your Job file on page 74. Write down any new words and phrases. You are in the reception area of the hotel where you work. Choose two places outside the hotel that guests ask directions to. Start from reception. Write out these directions for guests.

6.10   SPEAKING PRACTICE   *In pairs*

1   *Student A:* You are the guest. Go to page 100 and study Tapescript **6.7** exercise 1. Ask for directions to the five places mentioned: travel agent, bank, photo shop, cinema, cash point.

Student B: You are the employee. Go to page 100 and study Tapescript **6.7** exercise 1. Give the directions to your partner.

Change roles.

2   Take a map of your town. In pairs ask for and give directions to the two places you wrote directions to in your Job file. Change roles.

7 Room services

Part A *Hello, room service, can I help you?*

7.1 PRESENTATION

Look at this selection from the room service menu at Redz Bar and Brasserie at the Old Ship Hotel. How many of the dishes do you know? Do you serve any of these in the hotel where you work?

Old Ship Hotel, Brighton, UK

• **REDZ** •
BAR BRASSERIE

STARTERS

...... Grilled goat's cheese
...... Cajun salmon
...... Caesar salad
...... Smoked salmon

MAIN DISHES

...... Cod fillet
...... Pan-fried sesame salmon
...... Penne pasta
...... Grilled chicken
...... Sirloin steak

SIDE ORDERS

...... Garlic bread with mozzarella
...... Bruschetta
...... Mixed green salad
...... Chicken, bacon and brie baguette

PUDDINGS

...... Raspberry crème brûlée
...... Tiramisu
...... Apple strudel
...... Ice cream
...... Cheese board

7.2 LISTENING AND PRONUNCIATION

1 Two guests are ordering from room service.
Listen and write 1 (Guest 1) or 2 (Guest 2) next to the items each guest orders from the menu.

2 Two guests order from room service. The waiter brings each the wrong order.
Listen to the conversation between the guest and the waiter and write in the correct order.

Guest 1 The waiter brings: smoked salmon, green salad, and ice cream. The guest ordered:

Guest 2 The waiter brings: caesar salad, bruschetta, crème brûlée. The guest ordered:

3 Being clear and polite   Listen to these sentences and repeat them.

Hello, room service, can I help you?	And your room number, please?
That's the sesame salmon, isn't it?	Is that just one mixed salad?
So, that's the caesar salad, bruschetta, the sesame salmon, and the apple strudel.	That will be ready in about 15 minutes.
	Would you like anything else, madam?

7.3   LANGUAGE FOCUS AND PRACTICE

1   Checking language   In 7.2 you heard room service check the order. Study what they say.

Is that just one mixed salad?
So that's the chicken not the steak …
That's the sesame salmon, isn't it?
Would you like anything else?

Question: Is that …?
Affirmative: So that's …
Question tag: That's …, isn't it?
Final check: Would you like anything else?

2   A guest orders from room service. Read this conversation and complete the sentences.

ROOM SERVICE   Hello, room service, can I help you?

GUEST   We'd like a couple of light snacks, please. Is ....?

ROOM SERVICE   Yes, everything is on the menu.

GUEST   Then a light salad to start with, please.

ROOM SERVICE   Is ....?

GUEST   No, not the caesar, the mixed green salad, please. And one sesame salmon and the penne pasta … no dessert.

ROOM SERVICE   Would ....?

GUEST   No, nothing else, thank you. Oh, wait a moment, some garlic bread as well.

ROOM SERVICE   Right, so that's .... And what ....?

GUEST   Room 531.

ROOM SERVICE   It will ....

GUEST   About 15 minutes, good.

3   What question does the waiter need to ask to clarify the order?

7.4   PERSONAL JOB FILE

Go to your **Job file** on page 75 and write down any new words and phrases. List some of the most popular room service items in the hotel where you work. Complete the checking questions.

7.5   SPEAKING PRACTICE   *In pairs*

Student A: You are the guest. Go to pages 101–102 and study Tapescript **7.2** exercise **1**. Order from room service.
Student B: You are the employee. Go to pages 101–102 and study Tapescript **7.2** exercise **1**. Take the guest's order.

Change roles.

Part B *I'm sorry, it's not available at the moment.*

7.6 PRESENTATION

Here are some of the services offered by this hotel.

fitness centre   laundry service   meeting rooms
taking messages   swimming pool

Do you have any of these services in the hotel where you work? When are they available?

What do you say if the service is not available?

I'm sorry, it's closed at the moment.
I'm very sorry, it's not available now, but it opens tomorrow at 8 am.

Princess Sofia Intercontinental Hotel, Barcelona, Spain

7.7 LISTENING AND PRONUNCIATION

You will hear five conversations about hotel services between hotel employees and guests. Listen and complete the table. You have to do three things:

1 Match a service (A, B, etc.) to a guest (1, 2, etc.).
2 Say if the service is available or not. Write Yes or No.
3 Write down the time you hear for each service.

A Fitness centre   B Laundry service   C Meeting rooms   D Taking messages   E Swimming pool

	Guest 1	Guest 2	Guest 3	Guest 4	Guest 5
Service					
If available now					*No*
Time	*closed 5 pm*				

 2

> ### Being clear and polite
> Listen to these sentences and repeat them.
>
> I'm sorry, sir, but today is Saturday, and the laundry service closed at 5 pm.
>
> I'm afraid it closes at 6 pm.
>
> It's not possible to keep the meeting rooms open after 8 pm.
>
> It doesn't open until 8 am.
>
> Mrs Jones checked out this morning at 8.30.

"Room service, sir. You wanted someone to listen to your speech for the bankers' dinner."

7.8 LANGUAGE FOCUS AND PRACTICE

1 Apologising and giving reasons

In 7.7 you heard the hotel employees explaining that a service was not available, like this.

Apologising: I'm sorry, sir, the laundry service closed at 5 pm.
I'm afraid she checked out this morning.
(*Note:* You can say 'I'm very sorry', but you <u>can't</u> say 'I'm very afraid.')

Giving a reason: The meeting rooms close at 8 pm.
She checked out an hour ago.

2 Here are some reasons or explanations. Put the verbs in brackets in the past tense.

1 He .... at 9 am.   (leave)

2 She .... three times yesterday.   (call)

3 They .... this morning.   (check out)

4 The laundry service .... at 9 pm.   (close)

5 He .... here a few moments ago.   (is)

3 Answer these questions using your own words.

1 GUEST   Can we use the Business Centre from 9 am on Saturday?

    EMPLOYEE   (it opens at 10 am on Saturday)

    ----

2 GUEST   Is it OK to use the pool on Sunday evening?

    EMPLOYEE   (the pool closes at 6 pm on Sundays)

    ----

3 GUEST   The fitness centre seems to be locked at the moment. Why?

    EMPLOYEE   (it is now 6.30 am – it opens at 7 am)

7.9 PERSONAL JOB FILE

Go to your Job file on page 75 and write any new words and phrases. Which services are offered in the hotel where you work? What do you say if the service is not available? Correct the sentences. There are two mistakes in each.

7.10 SPEAKING PRACTICE *In pairs*

Student A: You are the guest. Go to page 88 and study the information in Speaking practice **7.10A**. Ask the hotel employee for the services you want.

Student B: You are the employee. Go to page 94 and study the information in Speaking Practice **7.10B** about opening and closing times of services. Answer the guest's questions using this information.

Change roles.

8 Problems & solutions

FOCUS: DEALING WITH A RANGE OF GUESTS' PROBLEMS, OFFERING SOLUTIONS, EXPLAINING HOW THINGS WORK

Part A *I'll see to it immediately.*

8.1 PRESENTATION

What problems do guests have in their rooms? Do they have problems with the TV, air-conditioning, heating, noise? What kinds of items do they forget to bring with them? Do they remember to bring shaving materials, nightgowns, hair dryers, etc.?

Look at the illustrations. Are these the kinds of problems guests have?

Can you think of any others?

8.2 LISTENING AND PRONUNCIATION

 Listen to five conversations between guests and hotel employees and match each guest and their problem.

	Problem
Guest 1	guest forgets razor and shaving cream
	sheets are dirty
Guest 2	
	mini-bar is empty
Guest 3	guest needs a hair dryer
	not enough hot water
Guest 4	
	no bulb in bedside lamp
Guest 5	more coathangers are needed

2

Being clear and polite   Listen to these sentences and repeat them.

Is there anything in particular you need, madam?

I'll send someone up right away.

I'll see to it immediately.

I'm very sorry, that shouldn't happen.

I'll contact housekeeping now.

I'll get someone to bring some up at once.

We can provide all these items.

8.3   LANGUAGE FOCUS AND PRACTICE

1   Solutions   Notice how the employee offers a solution to the guests' problem. The future with 'will' is used for a decision made at the time of speaking.

I'll send someone up right away.   (to send a person to a room)
I'll see to it immediately   (to do something, to act)
I'll contact housekeeping now.   (to call, tell, inform someone)
I'll get someone to bring some up.   (to tell someone to do something)

2   Complete these sentences using the correct words from the list.

send up   right away   contact them   provide   have   send one up   some more
I'll get   no   I'll bring it   ask

1   Could I .... some toothpaste and a toothbrush, please?
2   .... housekeeping to bring up some more towels ....
3   Can you .... a hair dryer, please?
4   That's no problem, madam, I'll .... right away.
5   There's .... shampoo or soap in the bathroom.

6   I'll .... maintenance to see to it at once.
7   We need .... coat hangers.
8   I'll .... at once.
9   Don't worry, sir, ... to your room myself.
10   We can .... those things for you, madam.

3   Look at these problems. What would you say? Write your answer.

1   GUEST   : We need some more towels in the bathroom.
    EMPLOYEE   : ---
2   GUEST   : I need to sew some buttons on to a shirt.
    EMPLOYEE   : ---
3   GUEST   : There's too much noise next door.
    EMPLOYEE   : ---

8.4   PERSONAL JOB FILE

Go to your Job file on page 76 and write down any new words and phrases. What problems do guests have in the hotel where you work? Note down a problem and the solution you would suggest.

8.5   SPEAKING PRACTICE   *In pairs*

Student A: You are the guest. Go to page 88 and study the information in Speaking practice **8.5A**. Explain each problem to the employee.

Student B: You are the employee. Go to page 94 and study the information in Speaking practice **8.5B**. Offer solutions to the guest.

Change roles.

Part B *You can choose your own code number for the safe.*

8.6 PRESENTATION

What kinds of problems do guests have with the amenities in the room?
Do guests have problems operating the TV or using the safe?

Here are two jumbled explanations. What do you think the correct order is?
There is more than one possibility. You will hear the answers in 8.7.

The TV

...... Press Play on the remote control

...... Choose a film

...... Sit back and enjoy the film

...... You will see a list of films

...... Press OK on the remote control

...... First switch on the TV

...... Then press Video on the remote control

The safe

...... Turn the dial quickly and the safe is locked

...... Put your valuables in and close the door

...... Remember this number; you'll need it to open the door again

...... Open the safe door

...... Tap A, then tap a six digit number, then tap C

...... On the front of the door you will see some letters and numbers

8.7 LISTENING AND PRONUNCIATION

1 Listen to a hotel employee explaining how the TV and the safe work.
Follow the instructions and write in the order you hear the steps explained.

2

> **Being clear and polite** Listen to the sentences from 8.7 exercise 1, and repeat them.

8.8 LANGUAGE FOCUS AND PRACTICE

1 Explaining how it works
Study these verbs. How many do you know?

turn on   turn off   turn up   turn down
press   tap in   key in   choose   open   close   put in   take out

Give an example of each one like this:

tap in   →   *Tap in the code number.*

2 What verbs would you use to explain how these things work?
From the list in 1 choose at least three verbs for each object. The first has been done for you.

Television   =   *turn on, turn off, choose*

Air-conditioning   = ...

In-room films   = ...

Mini-bar   = ...

Bedroom safe   = ...

3 Look at these photos. They explain how the keycard works. Write out the instructions.

Begin like this:

I'll show you, it works like this.

First ....

Then ....

....

Is that OK?

8.9   PERSONAL JOB FILE

Go to your Job file on page 76 and write down any new words and phrases.
Choose an appliance in the hotel that guests have trouble with. Explain how it works.

8.10   SPEAKING PRACTICE *In pairs*

1 *Student A:* Explain to your partner how to order a film on the TV. Then explain how the safe works.
Student B: Correct your partner. Insist on complete accuracy.

Change roles.

2 *Student A:* You are the guest. Go to page 88 and study the information in Speaking practice **8.10A**.
Explain the problems to your partner.
Student B: You are the employee. Go to page 94 and study the information in Speaking practice
8.10B. Suggest the best solution for each problem.

Change roles.

9 Taking bar orders

FOCUS: OFFERING; DESCRIBING WHAT IS AVAILABLE; DEALING WITH PAYMENT

Part A *What would you like to drink?*

9.1 PRESENTATION

What is the bar like in the hotel where you work?
Is it like any of these bars?

Look at the selection of drinks here. What drinks
are served in the bar at the hotel where you work?

Keio Plaza Hotel, Tokyo, Japan

9.2 LISTENING AND PRONUNCIATION

1 Some guests are ordering drinks.
Listen to the conversations between the guests and the bar person, and write down the orders.

Guest 1 .... Guest 3 .... Guest 5 ....

Guest 2 .... Guest 4 .... Guest 6 ....

2

Being clear and polite Listen to these sentences and repeat them.	
Good afternoon, madam, what would you like?	We have a wonderful local beer …
	We don't have that type of mineral water …
Good evening, sir, what can I get you?	… but we do have this one …
Would you like ice and lemon in the vodka?	Here you are, sir.

9.3 LANGUAGE FOCUS AND PRACTICE

1 Building the conversation
Study these stages of a conversation:

1	Welcome the guest	Good evening, madam.	....
2	Enquire	What would you like?	....
3	Explain the choice	We have a wonderful local beer.	....
4	Apologise	I'm sorry we don't have that whisky …	....
5	Offer an alternative	… but we do have this one.	....
6	Serve the drinks	Here you are, sir.	....

Study these six sentences. Each one is similar to one of sentences 1–6.
Write each sentence in the correct place on page 40.

… but we do have this natural water.   The house cocktail is excellent.
Your drinks, sir.   Good afternoon, madam.
What can I get you?   I'm afraid there's no more of that beer …

2 Look at this conversation between a bar person and a guest.
First complete the sentences using the words in the list.

very popular   are your   we don't have   can I get   you like ice
just some ice   draught beer   Good   I'd like   This

BAR PERSON	_1_	.... evening, madam.
BAR PERSON	......	Would .... and lemon in the coke?
GUEST	......	.... a large .... please, and a coke.
GUEST	......	OK, that's fine.
GUEST	......	No lemon, ... , please.
BAR PERSON	......	What .... you to drink?
BAR PERSON	......	Here .... drinks, madam.
BAR PERSON	......	I'm sorry, ... any draught beer.
BAR PERSON	......	.... local beer is ....
BAR PERSON	_9_	Certainly.

3 Now number these sentences 1–10 to put the conversation in the correct order.
Two have been done for you.

9.4 PERSONAL JOB FILE

Go to your Job file on page 77 and write down any new words and phrases. What are the
most popular drinks served in the hotel where you work? Write complete sentences for each
of the six stages of a dialogue between a bar person and guest.

9.5 SPEAKING PRACTICE *In pairs*

1 *Student A:* You are the guest.
        Go to page 104 and study Tapescript **9.2**.
        Practise ordering the drinks from **9.2** exercise **1**.
Student B: You are the bar person.
        Go to page 104 and study Tapescript **9.2**.
        Practise serving the drinks from **9.2** exercise **1**.

Change roles.

2 *Student A:* You are the guest.
        Go to page 88 and study the information in Speaking practice **9.5A**.
Student B: You are the bar person.
        Go to page 94 and study the information in Speaking practice **9.5B**.

Role play ordering and taking orders for drinks. Change roles.

Part B   *Shall I charge it to your room?*

9.6   PRESENTATION

How much are these drinks
in the hotel where you work?

A martini   A large whisky
A coke   A small glass of beer

How do guests pay for drinks
in the hotel bar?

They pay by Visa/credit card.
They pay by cheque.
They pay cash.
They charge it to their room.

	SINGLE	DOUBLE
Brandy	€7.50	€14.00
Whisky	€6.50	€12.00
Gin	€6.00	€12.00
Vodka	€6.00	€12.00
Rum	€6.00	€12.00
Martini	€5.50	€10.50
Draught beer	€3.00	€5.50
Bottled beer	€4.00	
Fruit juice	€3.00	
Tonic water	€2.00	
Coke	€2.00	
Mineral water	€2.00	

9.7   LISTENING AND PRONUNCIATION

1 Four guests are ordering drinks at a hotel bar. Listen to the conversations between the guests and the bar person, and complete the table. Write (Guest) 1, 2, 3 or 4 next to the correct order, method of payment and total.

Order	Payment method	Total
...... 2 large beers, 1 whisky, 1 vodka	...... Visa	...... €13.00
...... gin + tonic, coke, small beer	...... cheque	...... €23.50
...... double brandy, rum + coke, tonic	...... charge to room	...... €11.50
...... rum, dry martini	...... cash	...... €24.00

2

Being clear and polite   Listen to these sentences and repeat them.

Here you are, sir.

What can I get you, madam?

Shall I charge it to your room, madam?

Are you staying in the hotel?

Lemon with the gin, madam?

That comes to €11.50.

Could you sign here, please?

9.8 LANGUAGE FOCUS AND PRACTICE

1 Payment: Building the conversation
Notice the different ways of saying things.

The bill:	GUEST	Can I have the bill, please?
	GUEST	How much is it?
	BAR PERSON	That comes to £18.
Method of payment:	GUEST	Can I pay by credit card/cheque?
	BAR PERSON	Are you staying in the hotel?
	BAR PERSON	Shall I charge it to your room?
The tip:	GUEST	Please keep the change.
	BAR PERSON	Thank you sir/madam.

Study these three tenses.

We use the **present simple** to express general statements of no particular time: ➔ How much is it?

We use the **present continuous** to talk about things happening now or around now: ➔ Are you staying at the hotel?

We use '**Shall I**' for polite offers: ➔ Shall I charge it to your room?

2 Make complete sentences.

1	GUEST	Could / bill / please? _____
2	GUEST	How / it / come to? _____
3	GUEST	Can / pay / credit card? _____
4	BAR PERSON	€11.90 _____
5	GUEST	I / cash _____
6	BAR PERSON	guest / hotel? _____
7	BAR PERSON	charge / your room? _____
8	BAR PERSON	room / number? _____
9	GUEST	keep / change _____
10	BAR PERSON	Thank / much _____

9.9 PERSONAL JOB FILE

Go to your Job file on page 77 and write down any new words and phrases.
What currencies and methods of payment are used in the hotel where you work?
Write complete sentences for the three stages of a dialogue between the bar person and the guest: the bill, method of payment, and the tip.

9.10 SPEAKING PRACTICE *In pairs*

Student A: You are the guest. Go to page 88 and study the information in Speaking practice **9.10A**. There are six suggestions for drinks. Order these drinks.
Student B: You are the bar person. Take the six orders, ask about methods of payment, add up the total and present the bill.

Change roles.

10 In the restaurant (1)

Part A *Do you have a reservation?*

10.1 PRESENTATION

What do you say to guests when they arrive at the hotel restaurant? Now look at these situations. What would you say in each situation?

Read these dialogues. Match each one to an illustration.

1 WAITRESS : Here is the menu. Would you like an aperitif?
   GUEST : Yes, please.

2 GUEST : Could I have another martini, please?
   WAITRESS : Certainly. I'll bring it at once.

3 WAITRESS : Good evening. Do you have a reservation?
   GUEST : Yes, a table for two …
   WAITRESS : And your name, please?

4 GUEST : No, we don't have a reservation.
   WAITRESS : I'm sorry, we're fully booked tonight.

5 WAITRESS : Shall I take your coat?
   GUEST : Yes, thank you.

10.2 LISTENING AND PRONUNCIATION

🔊 1 Listen to five conversations between a waitress and guests and check your answers to 10.1.

🔊 2
> **Being clear and polite** Listen to these sentences and repeat them.
>
> Do you have a reservation?
>
> And your name, please?
>
> Shall I take your coat, madam?
>
> Here is the menu.
>
> Would you like an aperitif?
>
> Certainly, I'll bring it at once.
>
> I'm sorry, we're fully booked tonight.

A

B

C

D

E

10.3 LANGUAGE FOCUS AND PRACTICE

1 Greeting the guest

What do you say when you greet a guest at the hotel restaurant?
Correct these sentences. There is *one* mistake in each.

1 Do you have reservation?
2 How is your name, please?
3 Shall I have your coats?
4 There is the menu and wine list.
5 Do you like an aperitif?
6 I'm sorry, we're all booked this evening.

2 Building the conversation

Study these sentences.

O'Connor, yes, Mr O'Connor.   The name's O'Connor.   This way, please.
A non-smoking, by the window.   Here's your table by the window.   Yes, we have, a table for four.

Build a conversation using these sentences. Begin like this:

WAITER	Do you have a reservation?
GUEST	....
WAITER	....

Study these sentences.

So that's a fruit cocktail and a dry martini.   Yes, a dry martini …   Thank you.   Not for the moment.
… and a fruit cocktail, please.   Would you like anything else?

Build a conversation using these sentences. Begin like this:

WAITRESS	Can I get you an aperitif?
GUEST	....
WAITRESS	....
GUEST	....
WAITRESS	....

3 Find sentences that mean the same as:

Have you got a reservation? ....

Follow me, please. ....

10.4 PERSONAL JOB FILE

Go to your Job file on page 78 and write down any new words and phrases.
Which aperitifs are the most popular in the restaurant where you work?
Complete the conversation. The waiter is welcoming guests and taking orders for aperitifs.

10.5 SPEAKING PRACTICE *In pairs*

1 *Student A:* Go to page 105 and study Tapescript **10.2**.
Student B: Go to page 105 and study Tapescript **10.2**.

Practise the conversations with and without the tapescript. Change roles.

2 In the same way, practise the conversations you completed in 10.3 exercise 2.

Part B *Are you ready to order?*

10.6 PRESENTATION

Read these dialogues.
Match each one to an illustration.

A

B

1 **WAITRESS**   … and to follow, madam?
   GUEST   I'd like some fish to follow.
          What can you recommend?
   WAITRESS   The sole meunière is very good, madam,
          and very popular.

2 **WAITRESS**   How would you like the steak – rare,
          medium or well done?
   GUEST   Well done, please.

3 **WAITRESS**   So that's the waldorf salad and the sole
          meunière for madam, the medium steak
          for you, sir, a bottle of rosé and a bottle
          of sparkling mineral water. Thank you.

C

D

4 **WAITRESS**   Are you ready to order?
   GUEST   Yes, I am.

5 **GUEST**   What is the waldorf salad?
   WAITRESS   It's a crispy salad with cheese and croutons.
   GUEST   OK, I'll have that.

6 **WAITRESS**   And what would you like to drink?
   GUEST   How about a bottle of rosé? And a bottle
          of sparkling mineral water.

E

F

10.7 LISTENING AND PRONUNCIATION

1 Listen to the conversation between the waitress and guests and check your
answers in 10.6.

2

Being clear and polite
Listen to these sentences and repeat them.

Are you ready to order?

… and to follow, madam?

The sole meunière is very good and very popular.

How would you like the steak – rare, medium
or well done?

Would you like something to drink?

So that's the waldorf salad and the sole meunière,
medium steak, a bottle of rosé and a bottle of
sparkling mineral water.

~~ **Menu** ~~

STARTERS

Smoked Salmon … … … £8.50
Oysters … … £10.00
Waldorf Salad … … £8.50

~~~

MAIN COURSES

Rump or Fillet Steak … … £14.50
Roast Pork *in a Cream Sauce* … … £14.50
Whole Baked Trout … … £12.00
Sole Meunière … … £13.00
Steamed Turbot … … £12.00
Fried Prawns *with Mixed Salad* … … £11.00
Grilled Chicken *with Sautéed Onions* … £12.50

10.8 LANGUAGE FOCUS AND PRACTICE

1 Starters and the main course
Look at this menu for starters and the main course.

Check the meaning of these words.

smoked   baked   grilled   fried   sautéed   roasted   steamed

2   Study the way we build the conversation after greeting the guest and taking the order for the aperitif. Complete the conversation using the words in each list.

Starter   smoked   me   ready   salad

WAITRESS : Are you .... to order?

GUEST 1 : Yes, the .... salmon for me.

GUEST 2 : And the waldorf .... for ...., please.

Main dish (1) Asking and recommending   light   follow   turbot   some   how about   recommend

WAITRESS : … and to ...., madam?

GUEST 1 : I'd like .... fish but something .... What can you ....?

WAITRESS : The steamed turbot is very light, or .... the prawns and a salad?

GUEST 1 : The ...., please.

Main dish (2) Explaining a dish   try that   baked   fine   sole

GUEST 2 : What is the .... meunière?

WAITRESS : It's sole lightly .... in oil.

GUEST 2 : OK, that's ...., I'll ....

Choosing drinks   recommend   then   like   goes

WAITRESS : What would you .... to drink?

GUEST 1 : Can you .... a good wine, white preferably?

WAITRESS : Well, the Soave Classico Superiore .... very well with fish.

GUEST 1 : Good, a bottle of Soave ...., and a small bottle of mineral water.

Checking   bottle   steamed   that's   mineral

WAITRESS : So .... the sole meunière, the .... turbot, a bottle of Soave Classico
          Superiore, and a small .... of .... water. Thank you.

10.9   PERSONAL JOB FILE

Go to your Job file on page 78 and write down any new words and phrases.
Complete the conversation between the waitress and the guests.

10.10   SPEAKING PRACTICE *In pairs*

1   *Student A:* You are the waiter or waitress. Go to page 105 and study Tapescript **10.7**.
       Student B: You are the guest. Go to page 105 and study Tapescript **10.7**.

       Practise the conversation. Change roles.

2   Choose the best wine
       Work in groups of two or three: one waiter or waitress and two guests.

       Student A: You are the waiter or waitress. Go to page 89 and study the information in
                             Speaking practice **10.10A**. Select a wine to go with the guests' dishes, like this:
                             'The Côtes du Rhône goes very well with steak.'

       Students B and C: You are the guests. Choose several dishes from the menu in **10.8**, and ask the
                             waiter or waitress which wine they recommend with each dish.

       Change roles.

11 In the restaurant (2)

FOCUS: DEALING WITH ORDERS FOR DESSERTS AND COFFEE; PAYMENT

Part A *Would you like to see the dessert menu?*

11.1   PRESENTATION

What are the most popular desserts and cheeses in the hotel restaurant where you work?

Look at the lists below. Match each dessert and each cheese with the country it comes from.

Desserts		Cheeses	
Apple strudel	England	Brie	Holland
Trifle	Austria	Gouda	England
Chocolate soufflé	Italy	Cheddar	Switzerland
Tiramisu	France	Gruyère	France

11.2   LISTENING AND PRONUNCIATION

1 Study these two conversations between the waitress and guests. Put the sentences in the correct order to make the conversations.

GUEST 1	......	I'm afraid I'm full.
WAITRESS	......	Would you like to see the dessert menu?
WAITRESS	......	How was the fish, sir?
WAITRESS	......	Can I get you a coffee or a liqueur?
GUEST 1	......	Very good.
GUEST 1	......	Just an espresso, please. Oh, and the bill.

WAITRESS	......	It's a light cake with chocolate, biscuit, cream and marsala.
GUEST 2	......	Oh, just something light, what can you recommend?
WAITRESS	......	Would you like a dessert, madam?
WAITRESS	......	And for you, sir?
GUEST 2	......	The fruit salad sounds fine.
GUEST 3	......	What's tiramisu?
WAITRESS	......	How about the fresh fruit salad or some ice cream?
GUEST 3	......	OK, I'll try that.

Now listen and check your answers.

2 Two guests are ordering desserts, cheese and coffee. Listen and complete the order.

	Dessert	Cheese	Coffee
Man			
Woman		–	

DESSERTS

Fresh Fruit Salad £5.50

Apple Strudel £6.50

Trifle £7.00

Tiramisu £5.50

Chocolate soufflé £7.50

Selection of ice cream £6.00

SELECTION OF CHEESES

Brie, Gouda, Cheddar, Gruyère £4.50

COFFEE & TEA

Cappuccino, Espresso £2.00

Irish Coffee £4.00

Chinese Lotus Tea, Herbal Teas £2.00

3 **Being clear and polite** Listen to these sentences and repeat them.

Would you like to see the cheese tray?

Can I take your order for dessert?

The trifle is made with sherry.

The strudel is served hot with ice cream.

So that's an espresso and a cappuccino.

11.3 LANGUAGE FOCUS AND PRACTICE

Recommending items on the menu

In 11.2 the waitress recommended a dessert, like this:

WAITRESS : If you like chocolate, I can recommend the chocolate soufflé.

Here are some more possibilities:

WAITRESS : If you like very strong coffee, try the espresso.
If you prefer exotic tea, I suggest the Chinese lotus tea.

Now match A and B.

A	B
1 If you prefer a milky coffee,	try the Irish or English cheddar.
2 If you'd like something very English,	the fruit salad is very popular.
3 For a hard cheese,	try the cappuccino.
4 If you prefer something light,	I can recommend the sherry trifle.
5 The Irish coffee is just right	I suggest the apple strudel.
6 For a typically Viennese dessert,	if you like whiskey in your coffee.

11.4 PERSONAL JOB FILE

Go to your Job file on page 79. Write down any new words and phrases. Describe two of the most popular dessert dishes in the restaurant where you work. Say what they are and where they come from. Complete the suggestions using different expressions.

11.5 SPEAKING PRACTICE

1 **Explaining the desserts** *In pairs*

Look at these desserts and their ingredients.
In pairs ask and answer questions about the desserts, like this:

GUEST : What's the apple strudel?
WAITER/WAITRESS : It's pastry filled with apple and spices, baked, and served hot with ice cream.

Dish	Ingredients	Cooking method
Chocolate soufflé	eggs, cream, chocolate	baked, served cold
Fresh fruit salad	different fruits in season	mixed, served cold
Trifle	fruit, sponge cake, sherry, custard, cream	mixed, served cold
Tiramisu	eggs, biscuits, chocolate, marsala	set in layers, served cold
Apple strudel	apple, spices, pastry	baked, served hot

2 *In groups* One of you is the waiter/waitress, the others are guests. Go to page 105 and study Tapescript 11.2. Practise the conversation: ordering desserts, dealing with the order, explaining.

Change roles.

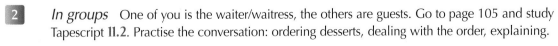

Part B *Was everything all right, sir?*

IL CAMPO RISTORANTE
Hotel Fratelli, 00126 Roma

PAGINA	NUMERO TAVOLO	TIPO DOCUMENTO	DATA DOCUMENTO	NUMERO
1	23	ric. fis.	23/07/2002	98

QUANTITÀ	DESCRIZIONE	IMPORTO €
1	Tonno e carciofini	14.50
1	Capricciosa	14.00
2	Acqua - 1 litro	6.00
2	Cappuccino	7.00
	TOTALE (IVA COMPRESA)	42.50

11.6 PRESENTATION

1 Look at this bill.

- Is it like a bill in the hotel restaurant where you work?
- On the bills you prepare is there a service charge?
- Is service included in the bill?
- Is tax included in the total?

2 What problems could there be with the bill?

- The total is wrong.
- An item was charged on the bill but not ordered by the guest.
- An extra service charge was added.

What is wrong with this bill? Correct the mistake.

3 Study these sentences. Decide who is speaking, one of the guests or the waitress. Write G(uest) or W(aitress) next to each sentence.

W Was everything all right, sir? *1*		We accept all types of credit cards. ......
...... Excuse me. Is this item correct?		...... The chocolate soufflé was delicious … ......
...... Oh, and can I pay by Visa?		...... I thought we had only one bottle of wine. ......
...... We hope to see you again.		...... Can I have the bill, please? ......
...... Is service included?		...... Here you are, we've corrected the mistake. ......
...... Yes, sir, it's included.		...... Oh, I'm very sorry, sir, I'll check that for you. ......

11.7 LISTENING AND PRONUNCIATION

1 Look at the sentences above again. Listen to the conversation between the waitress and the guests. They are talking about the meal and the bill, and then they say goodbye. Write in the order you hear the sentences above. The first has been done for you.

2 **Being clear and polite** Listen to these sentences and repeat them.

Was everything all right, sir?	We've corrected the mistake.
How was your meal?	Here's the correct bill, madam.
I'll check that for you.	Do come back again.
Excuse me, sir, I'll go and check.	We hope to see you again.

11.8 LANGUAGE FOCUS AND PRACTICE

1 Asking, and correcting a mistake

In 11.7 you heard the waitress do these three things:

A: Ask about the meal   B: Correct a mistake on the bill   C: Say goodbye

Study the sentences at each stage, A, B, and C.

A *Asking about the meal:*

WAITRESS : Was everything all right, sir? *How was your meal?*

WOMAN : The chocolate soufflé was delicious. ....

B *The bill:*

MAN : Is this item correct? ....

WAITRESS : I'll check that for you. ....

I'm very sorry. ....

We've corrected the mistake. ....

C *Saying goodbye:*

WAITRESS : We hope to see you again. ....

Study the sentences below. They are also about the meal, the bill and saying goodbye, but they are from a slightly different conversation.

Write each sentence by a sentence above to create a new conversation about the meal, the bill and saying goodbye. The first has been done for you.

Excuse me, sir, I'll go and check.   How was your meal?   Here's the correct bill, sir.
I don't think this is right.   Oh, I'm terribly sorry.   The soup was a little cold.
Do come back again.

2 You are the waiter/waitress. Reply to the guest.

1 GUEST : You've charged us for the cheese, but we didn't have any after all.

WAITER/WAITRESS : ....

2 GUEST : We only had one coffee, not two.

WAITER/WAITRESS : ....

3 GUEST : Is service included in the bill?

WAITER/WAITRESS : .... *(decide yourself)*

4 GUEST : Is VAT included in the total?

WAITER/WAITRESS : .... *(decide yourself)*

11.9 PERSONAL JOB FILE

Go to your Job file page 79. Write down any new words and phrases. Complete the sentences about the tip. Complete the conversation: ask about the meal, correct the bill, say goodbye.

11.10 SPEAKING PRACTICE *In groups*

1 One of you is the waiter/waitress, the others are guests. Go to page 106 and study Tapescript 11.7. Practise the conversation first with books open, then with books closed. Change roles.

2 Go to page 89 and study the complete menu. One of you is the waiter/waitress, the others are guests. Role play the situation using the menu.

Guests: Order a full meal, ask for suggestions.
Waiter/waitress: Take the orders, make suggestions, explain items on the menu, deal with payment, say goodbye.

Change roles.

12 Places to visit

FOCUS: SUGGESTING AND DESCRIBING PLACES TO VISIT

Part A   *Have you visited the Empire State Building?*

Empire State Building, New York

12.1   PRESENTATION

Which of these attractions do you have in your city or town?

museum   theatre   concert hall   famous monument
national park   art gallery   place of worship
famous building   city tour   special local attractions
(e.g. swimming with dolphins, firework displays)

Where do guests at your hotel want to visit?
What places do you recommend to guests?
Do you know how many of these famous sites
are in New York?

Statue of Liberty   Golden Gate Bridge
Rockefeller Center   Grand Central Station
The United Nations   Paul Getty Museum

LISTENING AND PRONUNCIATION

12.2

 1

Listen to some guests asking about places to visit in New York. Tick (✓) the places the hotel employee suggests to them.

	Guest 1	Guest 2	Guest 3
Art museum			
Theatre district			
Music concert			
Central Park			
Shopping in 5th Avenue			
Statue of Liberty			
City tour			
Empire State Building			

2

> **Being clear and polite**   Listen to these sentences and repeat them.
>
> New York is full of great places to visit.
> You must see it while you're here.
> You shouldn't miss the Empire State Building.
>
> You could go down to the theatre district on Broadway.
> I'll show you on this brochure …
> Why not go to the concert in Central Park?

12.3 LANGUAGE FOCUS AND PRACTICE

1 Suggesting places to visit

The guest asks about places to visit in New York.
Study the way the hotel employee makes suggestions like this.

GUEST : What do you suggest we visit?

EMPLOYEE : New York is full of great places to visit.
You must see it while you're here.
You shouldn't miss the Empire State Building.
You could go down to the theatre district on Broadway.
I'll show you on this brochure …
Why not go to the concert in Central Park?

2 Now complete the sentences below with the words in the list.

must go   could   is full of   shouldn't miss   why not   I'll show you   special   things

1 .... visit the United Nations while you are here?

2 You .... spend the afternoon in the Museum of Modern Art.

3 You .... to the free concert in Central Park.

4 The downtown district .... places to eat.

5 It's very near the hotel, here .... on the brochure.

6 You .... the view from the top.

7 Do you have any .... interests?

8 What kind of .... do you like?

12.4 PERSONAL JOB FILE

Go to your Job file on page 80. Write down any new words and phrases. Write down the interesting places to visit in your region. Write six recommendations you make to guests.

12.5 SPEAKING PRACTICE *In pairs*

1 *Student A:* You are the guest. Go to page 106 and study Tapescript **12.2**. Ask about places to visit.
Student B: You are the hotel employee. Go to page 106 and study Tapescript **12.2**. Tell the guest about interesting places to visit.

Practise the conversation first with the tapescript and then without. Change roles.

2 *Student A:* You are a guest at the Carlton Hotel on Madison Avenue in New York. Go to page 90 and study the list of interesting places to visit in New York. Ask the hotel employee for recommendations and directions.
Student B: You are the hotel employee at the Carlton Hotel on Madison Avenue in New York. Go to page 95 and study the street plan of New York showing some interesting places to visit. Answer the guest's questions. Make recommendations and give directions.

Change roles.

 THE CARLTON

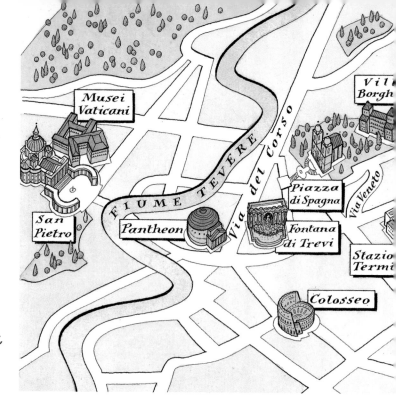

Part B *Rome is one of the most popular tourist spots in the world.*

12.6 PRESENTATION

In Part A, in your Job file 12.4, you wrote down the interesting places to visit in your region. You also wrote six recommendations of places to visit.

How do you compare these places? Do you say which is cheaper, busier, more expensive, more interesting?

12.7 READING AND COMPREHENSION

Read this article from a brochure about Rome.

A short break in Rome

Rome, called the Eternal City, founded over 2,700 years ago, is today one of the most popular tourist spots in the world, and for many people one of the most interesting. From a population of 200,000 a century ago, Rome now has over three million inhabitants.

For the visitor there is something to see and do for all tastes and all budgets. Rome is full of museums containing priceless works of art, beautiful monuments, piazzas, churches, and great places to eat.

There are of course many reasonably priced shops and restaurants but if you want a taste of the more expensive high fashion items, stroll up to the Via Veneto or along the Corso.

Right in the centre of Rome is the smallest state in Europe, the Vatican, but it contains the biggest church in the world, St Peter's. Here too you will find one of the largest museums in Rome and one of the most crowded, the Vatican Museum. Give yourself a day to get round it if you can.

A very popular tourist spot is the Spanish Steps (Piazza di Spagna), popular with tourists and locals alike. Another sight worth visiting is the historic Pantheon – older even than the Coliseum (Colosseo). And there is a beach, though it's about half an hour by car from the centre of the city.

Getting around even in summer, the busiest season, is not generally a problem, as long as you don't take the car. There are plenty of buses and taxis, and a metro too.

To see Rome in relative comfort, why not take a city bus tour around the most famous monuments? Tour buses leave Piazza dei Cinquecento, just in front of the railway station (Statione Termini), every day between 10.30 and 18.00. The tour takes $2\frac{1}{2}$ hours.

Buon viaggio.

Look at these questions and comparisons. Decide whether the comparatives are true or false, and if they are false correct them.

1 Is it busy?   Rome is busier during the winter than the summer.
2 Are the shops expensive? Shops in Via Veneto and the Corso are generally more expensive than elsewhere.
3 Is the beach far?   The beach is about half an hour by car from the city.
4 Is it crowded?   The Vatican Museum is not very crowded.
5 Is it popular?   The Spanish Steps is more popular with locals than with tourists.
6 Is it old?   The Coliseum is older than the Pantheon.

12.8 LANGUAGE FOCUS AND PRACTICE

1 Comparatives **Study these examples of comparatives.**

1 Is is *old*? The Pantheon is *older* than the Coliseum.

2 Is it *busy*? It's *busier* in summer than in winter.

3 Is it *crowded*? The Vatican Museum is *more crowded* than other museums.

4 Is it *expensive*? Shops in Via Veneto are *more expensive* than elsewhere.

There are three types of comparatives.
A: Short word = old – older   B: Short word ending in 'y' = busy – busier
C: Longer words = crowded – more crowded   interesting – more interesting

2 Study these adjectives. Which of the above groups do they fit in? Write A, B or C.

...... popular   ...... interesting   ...... sandy   ...... crowded   ...... exciting
...... modern   ...... safe   ...... relaxing   ...... big   ...... small   ...... far   ...... near

3 Answer these questions using a comparative adjective, like this.

Is it expensive? Yes, it's more expensive than the others.

1 Is it busy?   .... in summer than in winter.
2 Is it popular?   .... with young people than with older people.
3 Is it far?   .... than you think.
4 Is it exciting?   .... to see it live than to see it on TV.
5 Is it relaxing?   .... to travel by coach than to drive.
6 Is it safe?   .... to travel in a group than to travel alone.

4 Superlatives **Study these examples of superlatives.**

A: old – older – the OLDEST   B: busy – busier – the BUSIEST
C: crowded – more crowded – the MOST CROWDED

Answer these questions using a superlative adjective, like this.

Is it old?   Yes, it's one of the oldest. / No, it's one of the newest.

1 Is Rome a popular tourist spot?   Yes, it's one of .... in the world.
2 Is it busy in the summer?   Yes, summer is its .... season.
3 Is the Vatican State large?   No, it's one of .... in Europe.
4 Is St Peter's church small?   No, it's the .... in the world.
5 Is the Vatican Museum crowded?   Yes, it's one of the .... in Rome.

12.9 PERSONAL JOB FILE

Go to your Job file on page 80. Describe three places to visit in your region. Choose from the adjectives given and remember the forms.

12.10 SPEAKING PRACTICE *In pairs*

Student A: You are the guest. Ask your partner for information about interesting places to visit locally. Use these adjectives: interesting, sandy, modern, pretty, popular, busy, crowded, big, small, exciting, relaxing, safe, cheap, expensive.

Student B: You are the hotel employee. Suggest the guest visits three places you wrote about in your Job file in **12.9**. Answer the guest's questions about these places. Use the comparatives or superlatives of these adjectives as appropriate: interesting, sandy, modern, pretty, popular, busy, crowded, big, small, exciting, relaxing, safe, cheap, expensive.

Change roles.

13 Enquiries

Part A *The double rooms are from $240 to $280 a night.*

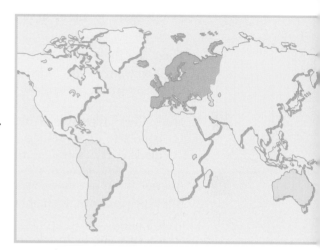

13.1 PRESENTATION

1 Match these currencies to countries in the world.

dollar yen pound euro franc yuan
rouble peso dinar rupee

In the hotel where you work what currencies do guests usually pay in?

2 Match the questions 1–4 with the appropriate answers A–D.

1 How much do the different rooms cost at the hotel where you work?
2 Why do prices vary?
3 What is included in the price?
4 What is not included in the price?

A mini-bar, airport shuttle
B room, taxes
C because some rooms have baths, some showers, some a sea view or a balcony
D between €120 and 170

13.2 LISTENING AND PRONUNCIATION

1 Three guests telephone three different hotels to enquire about room rates. Listen to the three conversations and complete the gaps.

The Stars Hotel	
Room	Rate
Single	US$ 220 – 250
Double / Twin	US$ .... – ....
Suite	US$ 550 – ....
A .... service charge applies to the above rates.	

The Devonshire Arms	
Room	Rate
Single	£ ....
Twin single occupancy (superior) £95	
Suite	£ ....
Rates are per room, per night and include full .... and	

Il Capello	
Room	Rate
Single	€180 – ....
Double / Twin	.... – €330
Breakfast	....
Extra bed	....
Tax and service charge included.	

2 Listen and circle the numbers you hear.

1 4 14 19 29 33 48 50 66 76 80 90 100 240 330 450 600 740 820 901 1,000

3

> **Being clear and polite** Listen to these sentences and repeat them.
>
> The double rooms are from $240 to $280 a night.
> The service charge is 15 per cent.
> The price includes a full English breakfast.
> VAT is included in the price.
>
> The rates have changed slightly since last year.
> The tax and the service charge are included.
> ... but the price doesn't include breakfast, which is €18.

13.3 LANGUAGE FOCUS AND PRACTICE

1 **Writing an answer**

The guest enquires about room rates. There are four parts in the answer.

A: Thanking the guest   B: Saying what is enclosed   C: Giving instructions   D: Offering further help

Study the language we use in each part.

A *Thanking the guest*

Thank you for ....

B *Saying what is enclosed*

Please find enclosed/attached a list of ....

C *Giving instructions*

Please notice the ....

If you wish to book by ....

Please include your ....

D *Offering further help*

If you need any more ....

Please don't hesitate ....

Study these words and phrases and use them to complete the sentences above.

credit card number and expiry date   information   high and low season rates
our room rates   to contact us   e-mail (or fax or letter)   your enquiry

2 Study this extract from an e-mail enquiring about room rates. Using the words and phrases in exercise 1 write an answer to this enquiry. Include the dates of the high and low season. Say if breakfast is included in the price. Decide these yourself.

> Would you please send me a full list of the room rates, including the dates of the high and low season rates?
>
> Is breakfast included in the room price? Thank you.
>
> Yours sincerely,
>
> Mary Hoffman

13.4 PERSONAL JOB FILE

Go to your Job file on page 81. Write down any new words and phrases. Write a brief letter to a guest answering his/her enquiry about room rates and offer to help with any further information.

13.5 SPEAKING PRACTICE *In pairs*

1
Student A: Go to page 90. Study the information in Speaking **13.5A** – the room rates of the Atlantic Hotel. Some of the information is missing.

Student B: Go to page 94. Study the information in Speaking practice **13.5B** – the room rates of the Atlantic Hotel. Some of the information is missing.

Ask and answer questions in order to complete the gaps in the information.

2
Student A: You are the hotel employee. Take a copy of the room rates of the hotel you work in.

Student B: You are the guest. Phone the hotel for information on room rates. Write down the information the hotel employee gives you.

Check your answers. Change roles.

Part B *We can supply all the latest audio-visual equipment.*

13.6 PRESENTATION

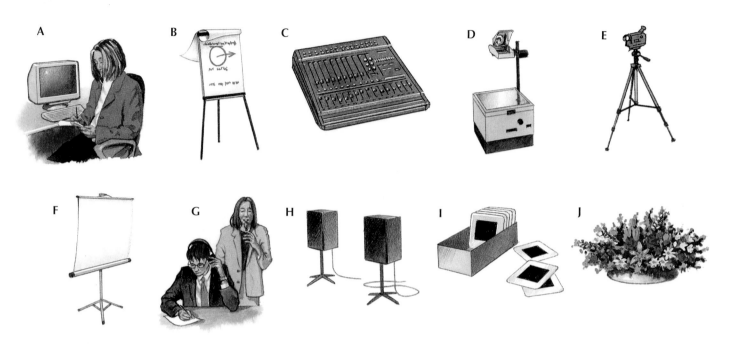

A B C D E

F G H I J

Look at this list of objects and label the illustrations.

loudspeakers   secretarial services   floral decoration   large screen   overhead projector
slides   simultaneous translators   flip chart   sound equipment   VCR equipment

13.7 LISTENING AND PRONUNCIATION

 1 You will hear two guests enquiring about conference facilities. Mark (Guest) 1 or (Guest) 2 next to the facilities each guest asks for. Which two items below are *not* mentioned?

...1... overhead projectors   ...... sound equipment   ...... loudspeakers

...... secretarial services   ...... large screens   ...... slides

...... flip charts   ...... simultaneous translators ...... floral decoration

...... VCR equipment

2

Being clear and polite   Listen to these sentences and repeat them.

Certainly, sir, we can do that for you.	We have a full team of translators.
Our meeting rooms have a very relaxed atmosphere.	If it's not in the hotel we can certainly arrange to get it.
We can seat up to 80 people.	We have several different arrangements we can offer.
We have all the latest audio-visual equipment.	

13.8 LANGUAGE FOCUS AND PRACTICE

1 Answering an enquiry
Study this letter. Could the hotel where you work satisfy this request?

2 Identify the main points to answer by completing the information below.

Room: *for up to 150 people*

Dates: _____

Equipment: _____

Translations: _____

Other: _____

3 Answer the letter using the correct words from the list.

up to 150   contact me   busy weekend   look forward   your enquiry   book early
simultaneous translation   conference pack   special rates   conference rooms

Dear Sir/Madam,

Would you please send me details concerning your conference and meeting facilities?

We need a very versatile room for up to 150 people for the weekend of November 3–5. Would you let me know if you could provide the following facilities:

- overhead film projectors, flip charts, sound equipment, large screens
- simultaneous translations in English, French and Italian

Would you also please send me a full price list?

I look forward to hearing from you.

Yours sincerely,

Keiko Wan

Dear Keiko Wan,

Thank you very much for _____ concerning our facilities. We would be very happy to accommodate you in one of our many _____, arranged to suit your needs. The rooms are very versatile and can easily accommodate _____ people.

The weekend of 3–5 November will be a very _____ due to the November Festival, so I would advise you to _____.

We provide a full range of audio-visual facilities and a full _____ service. Please find enclosed our _____, giving full details of all the conference services, including prices, plus details of our _____.

If you require any further assistance, please _____ directly and I will deal with your enquiry immediately.

I _____ to hearing from you.

Yours sincerely,

13.9 PERSONAL JOB FILE

Go to your Job file on page 81. Write down any new words and phrases. Write a brief letter to a guest answering his/her enquiry about conference facilities in the hotel where you work.

13.10 SPEAKING PRACTICE *In pairs*

1 *Student A:* You are the guest. You want to enquire about conference facilities. Go to page 90 and study the information in Speaking practice **13.10A**. Ask the hotel employee for what you need.

Student B: You are the hotel employee. Could the hotel where you work satisfy the guest's requirements? Use the conference pack from the hotel where you work to answer the guest's enquiries.

Change roles.

2 *In groups* There are 10 main items in the Presentation in **13.6**. Choose the six essential items a good conference centre should have. Explain your choice to the class.

14 Using the phone

FOCUS: DEALING WITH ROOM BOOKINGS AND MESSAGES BY PHONE

Part A *Good morning, Plaza Hotel, can I help you?*

14.1 PRESENTATION

1 What does an employee say when answering a phone call from outside?

Good morning / good evening, Plaza Hotel, can I help you?

Hello, Plaza Hotel, can I help you?

Hi, Plaza Hotel.

2 What does an employee say when finishing a phone call?

Goodbye.

Have a good day.

Thank you for calling.

14.2 LISTENING AND PRONUNCIATION

1 A guest phones the Plaza Hotel to book a room.
The hotel can't satisfy the request. The employee offers an alternative.

Listen to the conversation between the employee and the guest and circle the correct answer.

The guest wants to book: single room   double room   suite

with bath   with shower

for 2 nights   3 nights   4 nights

from 9   19   29 March

to 13   22   31 March

The guest accepts: single room   double room   suite

The room will be held until: 5 pm   6 pm   7 pm

2

Being clear and polite Listen to these sentences and repeat them.
What kind of room would you like?
Yes, madam, for how many nights?
We have no more singles for that weekend.
There are some doubles left.
Could you please confirm that by fax or e-mail?
We'll need a credit card number and expiry date, please.
We'll hold the room until 6 pm.
We look forward to seeing you on the 19th.

14.3 LANGUAGE FOCUS AND PRACTICE

1 Building the conversation

A guest phones to book a room. The employee apologises as the hotel can't satisfy the request, and then offers an alternative. Study the three stages, A, B, C.

A *Request:*   A guest phones the hotel to book a room.

B *Apology:*   The hotel can't satisfy the request.

C *Alternative:* The employee offers an alternative.

Study the language at each stage, A, B, C.

A *Request:*   Hello, I'd like a single room from the 19th to the 22nd March.

B *Apology:*   I'm sorry we have no more singles for that weekend.

C *Alternative:* There's just one double left.

2 This is part of the tapescript you heard in **14.2**. Complete the sentences by writing the correct word in the spaces. Choose these words yourself.

EMPLOYEE	I'm very ...., madam, but we .... no .... singles for that weekend.
GUEST	Oh, that's a pity. .... you have any doubles ....?
EMPLOYEE	Let me see, yes, madam, ... just one double left.
GUEST	And how much ....?
EMPLOYEE	.... $130 per night, not .... breakfast.
GUEST	I see, and the single is $95. OK, ... better .... the double then.
EMPLOYEE	Right, madam, and your ...., please?
GUEST	It's Mrs Delaporte, that's D-E-L-A-P-O-R-T-E.
EMPLOYEE	Could you please .... that by fax or e-mail, Mrs Delaporte, and we'll need a .... card number and .... date, please.
GUEST	Of course.

14.4 PERSONAL JOB FILE

Go to your Job file on page 82. Write down any new words and phrases. Write down how you begin, and end a telephone conversation in the hotel where you work. Write a brief conversation between a hotel employee and guest where the hotel can't offer the guest what they want, but have an alternative.

14.5 SPEAKING PRACTICE *In pairs*

1 *Student A:* You are the guest. Go to page 108 and study Tapescript **14.2**.
Student B: You are the employee. Go to page 108 and study Tapescript **14.2**.

Practise the conversation, first with books open, then books closed. Change roles.

2 *Student A:* You are the guest. Go to page 90 and study the information in Speaking practice **14.5A**.
Student B: You are the employee. Go to page 95 and study the information in Speaking practice **14.5B**.

Role play the conversation about booking a room by phone. Change roles.

Part B *I'm afraid the line is busy, would you like to hold?*

14.6 PRESENTATION

Here are four situations an employee deals with on the phone.

1 A caller asks to speak to a guest in room 23.
2 The employee calls the room but the line is busy.
3 The employee offers to take a message.
4 The guest asks to leave a message.

What would an employee say in each case?

A I'm sorry there's no answer. Can I take
   a message?
B Room 23, I'll put you through.
C Certainly, I'll make sure they get the message.
D I'm afraid the line is busy.

Match the situations with the sentences.

14.7 LISTENING AND PRONUNCIATION

1 Four different callers are phoning the Plaza Hotel. Listen to the four conversations and complete the message notes.

TELEPHONE MESSAGE

For ....
Room number ....
From ....
Message ————————
....
....
....
....
....

TELEPHONE MESSAGE

For ....
Room number ....
From ....
Message ————————
....
....
....
....
....

TELEPHONE MESSAGE

For ....
Room number ....
From ....
Message ————————
....
....
....
....

TELEPHONE MESSAGE

For ....
Room number ....
From ....
Message ————————
....
....
....
....

2

Being clear and polite Listen to these sentences and repeat them.	
I'm afraid the line is busy, would you like to hold?	Would you like to leave a message?
I'll put you through.	Could you spell that, please?
There's no answer, can I take a message?	I'll make sure he gets the message.
Just connecting you …	I'll give her the message as soon as she returns.

14.8 LANGUAGE FOCUS AND PRACTICE

1 Taking messages Study these verbs.

One-word verbs: to leave (a message)   to take (a message)   to give (a message)
Two-word verbs: to put someone through   to call back   to hold on

2 Complete the dialogues below by writing the correct words in the gaps.
Choose these words yourself.

1

EMPLOYEE Hello, Plaza Hotel, ... I help you?
CALLER Yes, can you .... me .... to Rosemary James, it's room 213.
EMPLOYEE I'm afraid the .... is busy, would you like to ....?
CALLER OK, I'll ....
EMPLOYEE The line's still ...., I'm afraid.
CALLER In that case I'll .... a message.

2

CALLER Good morning, can I .... room 87, please?
EMPLOYEE I'm afraid there's no ...., can I .... a message?

3

CALLER Can I .... to Pierre Chatry in suite 2, please?
EMPLOYEE Right, madam, I'll .... you ....
There's .... answer, would you like to .... a message?

4

EMPLOYEE Hello, Plaza Hotel, can I help you?
CALLER Yes, can you .... me .... to Jane Campbell in room 101?
EMPLOYEE Just .... you. ... I'm sorry, madam, but there's .... reply from her room.
CALLER Can I .... a message?
EMPLOYEE Yes, of course.
CALLER Tell her to .... the office as soon as possible.
EMPLOYEE Certainly, I'll .... her the message as soon as she returns.
CALLER Thank you.

14.9 PERSONAL JOB FILE

Go to your Job file on page 82. Write down any new words and phrases.
Write down what an employee, answering the phone, would say in each of the situations.

14.10 SPEAKING PRACTICE *In pairs*

1 *Student A:* You are the caller. Go to pages 108–9 and study Tapescript **14.7**.
Student B: You are the employee. Go to pages 108–9 and study Tapescript **14.7**.

Practise the conversation. Change roles.

2 *Student A:* You are the caller. Go to page 90 and study the information in Speaking practice **14.10A**.
Student B: You are the employee. Go to page 95 and study the information in Speaking practice **14.10B**.

Role play the situation. Change roles.

15 The check-out

Part A *How would you like to pay?*

15.1 PRESENTATION

What would you say to a guest who is checking out and paying the bill?

Match A and B to make complete sentences.

A	B
How would	the mini-bar today?
Have you used	you like to pay?
Everything is	charge is 10%.
How will you	included.
The service	be paying?

How do guests usually pay at the hotel where you work?

by cheque   by credit card   by account   in cash

15.2 LISTENING AND PRONUNCIATION

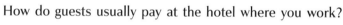 Four guests are checking out of the Ocean Hotel. They are paying their bills. Listen to the conversations between the guests and the hotel employee. Circle the correct answers.

Guest 1

He pays by:	cheque account credit card traveller's cheque
His bill comes to:	€417 €463 €470 €473
Service included:	yes no

Guest 3

He pays by:	credit card cheque cash account
His bill comes to:	€893 €918 €983 €988
Also on the bill:	meeting rooms breakfasts

Guest 2

She pays by:	credit card cheque account cash
Her bill comes to:	€319 €359 €390 €399
ID is a:	bank guarantee card passport nothing

Guest 4

She pays by:	credit card cash cheque traveller's cheque
Her bill comes to:	€223 €230 €232 €320
She leaves a tip:	yes no

 Being clear and polite   Listen to these sentences and repeat them.

Your bill is ready, sir.	We'll need some identification.
How would you like to settle your account?	Would you just sign here, please?
It comes to €390, madam.	And here is your receipt.

15.3 LANGUAGE FOCUS AND PRACTICE

1 Present perfect

Study the three parts of the verb 'use': use – used – used. Notice the past participle 'used'. This is how we form the present perfect: Have you used ...?

Study what the hotel employee says, and the answer:
Question: Have you used the mini-bar today?   *Answer:* Yes, I have. / No, I haven't.

One function of the present perfect is to express a past event that has an important consequence *now* or *around now*, for example:

Mr Jones has just left the hotel. = So I can't contact him <u>now</u>.
Have you got everything? = You mustn't forget anything. You need to have everything with you <u>now</u>.

2 Study the verb list on page 111. Write the past participles of these verbs.

leave .... finish .... do .... pay ....

make .... get .... expire .... put ....

Put the past participle of the verb into the correct place in each sentence.

1 Have you it yet?   do   5 I think you have a mistake.   make
2 Has Mrs Wilson the hotel yet?   leave   6 Have you your tickets?   get
3 Have you my luggage on the bus?   put   7 Has he the bill?   pay
4 She hasn't packing yet.   finish   8 I think this credit card has.   expire

3 Put the words in these *questions* in the correct order.

1 done Have everything you

.... ?

2 you identification any Have got any

.... ?

3 checked Has out she yet

.... ?

4 yet he bill paid Has the

.... ?

Put the words in these *answers* in the correct order.

A out Yes checked just she's

....

B hasn't No he

....

C are have Yes you I here

....

D haven't No yet I

....

Now match the questions and answers.

15.4 PERSONAL JOB FILE

Go to your Job file on page 83. Write down any new words and phrases. Write the questions in exercise 1 and write the answers in exercise 2.

15.5 SPEAKING PRACTICE *In pairs*

1 *Student A:* You are the guest. Go to page 109 and study Tapescript **15.2**.
Student B: You are the hotel employee. Go to page 109 and study Tapescript **15.2**.

Practise the dialogues first with books open, then books closed. Change roles.

2 *Student A:* You are the guest. Go to page 91 and study the information in Speaking practice **15.5A**.
Student B: You are the hotel employee. Go to page 96 and study the information in Speaking practice **15.5B**.

Role play the conversation between the hotel employee and guest. Change roles.

Part B *That's the 10% service charge in lieu of gratuities.*

15.6 PRESENTATION

Look at this hotel bill. Is it like a bill in the hotel where you work? What's the same? What's different?

The guest who wants to ask about items on the bill may say:

Can you explain this item, please?
What's this charge for?

The hotel employee may say:

This is the separate dry cleaning charge.
Here are the details of the calls you made.
I'm sorry, this is our mistake.

What questions do guests ask about the bill? What do you reply?

DATE	TIME	DESCRIPTION	AMOUNT	BALANCE
05/09		LOBBY LOUNGE	$37.50	$37.50
		ROOM CHARGE	$230.00	$267.50
	17.31	PRESSING	$14.00	$281.50
	17.31	DRY CLEANING	$14.00	$295.50
	17.32	LAUNDRY	$19.00	$314.50
	17.33	SERVICE CHARGE	$23.00	$337.50
06/09		ROOM CHARGE	$230.00	$567.50
	12.16	MINI-BAR	$39.00	$606.50
	06.41	OVERSEAS CALL	$12.00	$618.50
	18.54	TRANSPORTATION	$25.00	$643.50

15.7 LISTENING AND PRONUNCIATION

1 Listen and circle the numbers you hear.

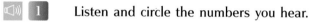

2 12 23 29 37 41 54 66 78 99 120 230 370 456 590 682 736 928 4,000 7,500 14,470

2 A guest is asking the hotel employee questions about the bill. Listen to the conversation and number these sentences in the order you hear them. The first and last have been done.

GUEST	_1_	Could you explain these items on my bill, please?
EMPLOYEE	.....	That's the usual practice, the laundry is charged separately.
EMPLOYEE	.....	Is everything OK now, madam?
GUEST	.....	Why are there two charges for dry cleaning and laundry?
EMPLOYEE	.....	I'll check again.
EMPLOYEE	.....	That's the 10% service charge in lieu of gratuities.
EMPLOYEE	.....	Yes, our records show you made three calls overseas.
GUEST	.....	Oh, I see. And did I really make three phone calls overseas?
GUEST	.....	Oh, did I really?
EMPLOYEE	.....	Certainly, madam, what would you like to know?
GUEST	.....	But what's this 10% charge?
GUEST	_12_	Yes, I think so.

3

Being clear and polite Listen to these sentences and repeat them.
What would you like to know?
That's the usual practice.
That's the 10% service charge in lieu of gratuities.
That's for the car you ordered last week.
Is everything OK now, sir?
I hope you enjoyed your stay.
Have a good day, madam, and we hope to see you again.

15.8 LANGUAGE FOCUS AND PRACTICE

1 Queries on the bill; the past tense

Study the language when the guest queries items on the bill and when the hotel employee explains these items. Look at the way the past tense is used in these sentences.

GUEST	Could you explain these items on my bill, please?
EMPLOYEE	That's for the car you ordered last week.

GUEST	I thought I only made two calls.
EMPLOYEE	Our records show you made three calls.

2 Study the verb list on page 111. Write the past tense of these verbs.

think ....   phone...............   pay ....   make ....   have ....

go ....   expire...............   order ....   leave ....   is ....

Put the verb(s) given into the correct place in each sentence, using the past tense.

1   **GUEST** : What's this transportation charge for, please?
    EMPLOYEE : That, madam, is for the car you .... last week.   order

2   **GUEST** : I .... we only .... two drinks from the mini-bar.   think / have
    EMPLOYEE : I'll just check that.

3   **GUEST** : I .... that we .... London only once.   think / phone
    EMPLOYEE : Here are the details of the two calls you ....   make

4   **GUEST** : I'm sure I .... for the drinks in the lounge.   pay
    EMPLOYEE : I'm sorry, madam, you're right, that's our mistake.

5   **EMPLOYEE** : I think your credit card .... last month.   expire
    GUEST : Oh, I'm sorry, in that case I'll pay by cheque.

6   **EMPLOYEE** : Our records show you .... breakfast from room service.   order
    GUEST : Oh, I ....?   do

7   **EMPLOYEE** : I hope you .... your stay.   enjoy
    GUEST : Yes, thank you.

15.9 PERSONAL JOB FILE

Go to your Job file on page 83. Write down any new words and phrases. Answer the questions from the guest. Decide yourself on the appropriate answers. Write down how you say goodbye to guests leaving the hotel.

15.10 SPEAKING PRACTICE *In pairs*

1 *Student A:* You are the guest. Go to page 110 and study Tapescript **15.7**.
Student B: You are the hotel employee. Go to page 110 and study Tapescript **15.7**.

Practise the dialogues first with books open, then books closed. Change roles.

2 *Student A:* You are the guest. Go to page 91 and study the information in Speaking practice **15.10A**.
Student B: You are the employee. Go to page 96 and study the information in Speaking practice **15.10B**.

Role play the conversation between the employee and the guest, who is asking questions about the bill. Change roles.

3 Saying goodbye Look at the last sentence you wrote in 15.8: 'I hope you enjoyed your stay.' In pairs, employee and guest, say goodbye to each other. Which of these expressions would you also use when saying goodbye to a guest?

Thank you for choosing our hotel.   Have a good trip.   Bon voyage.   See you next year.

Personal job file

HOW TO USE THE JOB FILE

The Job file is for you. Each student's Job file will be different, and will be a personal record of the language that is most useful in your work.

- Study the tips below.
- Write down all the new words and phrases from the lesson that are most useful to you.
- Write as many personal examples as you can in the Job file exercises.
- Revise your work regularly.
- Keep the Job file as a personal record of the language you need for your work.

STUDY TIPS

1   Look up English words in a good bilingual dictionary, e.g.
    waiter – garçon de café, serveur
    waitress – serveuse

    Then write the English word and the translation in your **Job file**.

2   Learn the pronunciation and the stress, e.g. *re'ceptionist.*

3   Use a personal example of a word, e.g.
    I'm a <u>receptionist</u> at the Plaza Hotel.

4   Group relevant words together, e.g.
    bed   sheet   pillow   pillowcase   duvet   blanket

5   Draw a picture to help you remember a word, e.g.
    bed

6   Learn adjectives and nouns together, e.g.
    a private beach

7   Make questions from statements, e.g.
    I work at the Ritz.
    Question: Where do you work?

8   Learn opposites, e.g.
    BIG – small   ↑go up – go down↓

Personal job file

1 Introductions

New words and phrases:

....	Translation	....
....	Translation	....
....	Translation	....
....	Translation	....
....	Translation	....

1.4 Here are two answers. Write the two questions.

Q: .... A: My name's Pablo.

Q: .... A: I'm a waiter.

Here are two questions. Write the two answers:

Q: What's your name? A: ....

Q: What do you do? A: ....

1.9 Complete this dialogue.

A Hello, my name's .... I'm .... I'm a .... I work in the
.... Hotel. And you, ...?

B Hi ...., my .... Maria.

A Hi .... Nice to meet you, Maria. Where .... from?

B Spain.

A Oh, what part?

B Madrid.

A And what .... you do?

Personal job file

New words and phrases:

....	Translation ....
....	Translation ....
....	Translation ....
....	Translation ....
....	Translation ....

2.4   **1**   **Write these dates.**

Today's date .... Your birthday ....

What other dates are important to you? ....

....

2   **Confirmation letter** **Fill in the gaps using your own words.**

Dear ....,

We are .... to confirm your ....

Arrival .... Departure ....

Room .... Rate ....

Confirmation ....

We look forward to .... on ....

Kind regards,

2.9   **A guest is checking in. Complete the dialogue using your own words.**

RECEPTIONIST   Good evening, sir, can I .... you?

GUEST   Good evening. I'm afraid I don't have a ....

Do you .... a double .... for tonight?

RECEPTIONIST   I'll just .... Yes, we have a .... room with twin beds and bath.

GUEST   And how much is it?

RECEPTIONIST   It's 190 euros per .... for the room, not including breakfast.

GUEST   That's ...., I'll take it.

Personal job file

3 The hotel bedroom

New words and phrases:

....	Translation ....
....	Translation ....
....	Translation ....
....	Translation ....
....	Translation ....

3.4 Describe a standard bedroom in the hotel where you work using some of these words:

TV   double bed   sheets   CD player   coat hangers   wardrobe
desk   chairs   radio alarm   remote control   pillows   telephone

....

....

....

....

....

....

3.9 Describe a luxury bedroom in the hotel where you work using some of these words:

mini-bar   blanket   duvet   bedside lamp   suitcase stand   dressing table
central light switch   trouser press   laundry bag   air-conditioning
writing paper   flowers   plants   personal safe

....

....

....

....

....

....

Personal job file

4 Bathroom & porter

New words and phrases:

-- Translation --

-- Translation --

-- Translation --

-- Translation --

-- Translation --

4.4 Describe a bathroom in the hotel where you work using some of these words:

bath   shower   washbasin   soap   hot   cold water   toilet paper   towels
mirror   shampoo   tissues   light switch   shaver socket   bathrobe   bin
next to   under   in   on   over   behind

4.9 Complete the three stages of this conversation:

1   *In the lobby*

PORTER   :   Can I --

GUEST   :   Yes, please --

2   *Leaving the lobby*

PORTER   :   This way --

GUEST   :   --

3   *At the guest's room*

PORTER   :   --

GUEST   :   --

PORTER   :   --

Personal job file

5 Services in the hotel

New words and phrases:

-- Translation --

-- Translation --

-- Translation --

-- Translation --

-- Translation --

5.4   **1**   **Correct the mistakes in each question and answer.**

Q: What time the restaurant is open, please?   A: It open at 7 pm.

Q: Laundry service still is available?   A: I'm sorry, it is close at 10 pm.

2   **Write four questions and answers about opening and closing times of services at the hotel where you work.**

Question   Answer

1 --   --

2 --   --

3 --   --

4 --   --

5.9   Write four questions and answers about business and leisure services at the hotel where you work.

Question   Answer

1 --   --

2 --   --

3 --   --

4 --   --

Personal job file

New words and phrases:

.... Translation ....

.... Translation ....

.... Translation ....

.... Translation ....

.... Translation ....

6.4 You are in the reception area of the hotel where you work. Choose four places guests want to go to inside the hotel. Start from reception. Write down these four directions for guests.

1 ....

....

2 ....

....

3 ....

....

4 ....

....

6.9 You are in the reception area of the hotel where you work. Choose two places outside the hotel that guests ask directions to. Start from reception. Write down these directions for guests.

1 ....

....

2 ....

....

Personal job file

New words and phrases:

---------------------------------- Translation --

---------------------------------- Translation --

---------------------------------- Translation --

---------------------------------- Translation --

---------------------------------- Translation --

7.4 **1** List some of the most popular room service items in the hotel where you work.

1 _____ 3 _____

2 _____ 4 _____

2 Complete these checking questions. There is one guest. The full order is:
1 salad, 1 vanilla ice cream, 1 black coffee.

Question: Is that _____? *(check caesar or mixed green)*

Affirmative: So that's _____
_____ *(repeat order)*

Question tag: That's _____, isn't it? *(confirm it's an espresso)*

Final check: Would you like _____?

7.9 **1** Which services are offered at the hotel where you work? What do you say if the service is not available?

----

2 Correct these sentences. There are *two* mistakes in each.
1 It's doesn't open 8 am.
2 I'm very sorry, sir, but swimming pool closes 10 pm.
3 Is not possible use the fitness centre after 8 pm.
4 I'm very afraid it's no open now.
5 Mrs Jones checks out yesterday 8.30.

Personal job file

8 Problems & solutions

New words and phrases:

--- Translation --

--- Translation --

--- Translation --

--- Translation --

--- Translation --

8.4 What problems do guests have in the hotel where you work? Note down one problem and the solution you would suggest.

GUEST

EMPLOYEE

8.9 Choose an appliance in the hotel that guests have trouble with. Explain how it works.

It works like this --

Personal job file

9 Taking bar orders

New words and phrases:

.... Translation ....

.... Translation ....

.... Translation ....

.... Translation ....

.... Translation ....

9.4 **1** What are the most popular drinks served in the hotel where you work?

....

2 Write complete sentences for each of these six stages of a dialogue between a bar person and guest.

1 Welcome the guest ....

2 Enquire about drinks ....

3 Explain choice ....

4 Apologise that the drink is not available ....

5 Offer an alternative ....

6 Serve the drinks ....

9.9 **1** What currencies and methods of payment are used in the hotel where you work?

....

2 Write complete sentences for these three stages of a dialogue between a bar person and guest: the bill, method of payment, and the tip.

1 Guest asks for the bill. You present it.

GUEST ....

BAR PERSON ....

2 Guest asks about payment. You explain.

GUEST ....

BAR PERSON ....

3 The tip

GUEST ....

BAR PERSON ....

Personal job file

10 In the restaurant (1)

New words and phrases:

....	Translation	....
....	Translation	....
....	Translation	....
....	Translation	....
....	Translation	....

10.4 **1** Which aperitifs are the most popular in the restaurant where you work?

....

2 Complete this conversation. The waiter is welcoming guests and taking orders for aperitifs.

WAITER : Good .... reservation?

GUEST : Yes, ... The name's ....

WAITER : Yes, ... Follow .... Here ....
an aperitif?

GUEST : Yes, a .... and a ....

WAITER : So, that's ....

10.9 Complete the conversation between the waitress and the guests.
Remember the stages: asking and recommending, explaining, choosing, checking.

WAITRESS : What .... follow, sir?

GUEST 1 : Some fish, please, ... recommend?

WAITRESS : The ....

GUEST 1 : OK, I'll have that, please.

WAITRESS : And you, madam?

GUEST 2 : Could you tell me what this meat dish is, please?

WAITRESS : Yes, the .... It's ....

GUEST 2 : I'll try it, and .... red wine.

WAITRESS : May I recommend the ....

GUEST 1 : Sounds good.

GUEST 2 : And a .... of sparkling ...., please.

WAITRESS : So, that's .... Thank you.

Personal job file

New words and phrases:

.... Translation ....

.... Translation ....

.... Translation ....

.... Translation ....

.... Translation ....

11.4 **1** Describe two of the most popular dishes in the restaurant where you work. Say what they are and where they come from.

1 ....

2 ....

2 Complete the suggestions using these expressions:
Try the ...   I can recommend the ...   I suggest ...

1 If you prefer herbal tea, ...

2 If you like cooked desserts, ...

3 For a soft cheese, ...

4 If you prefer something cold, ...

5 For something very traditional   ....

6 If you prefer coffee with whiskey, ...

11.9 **1** Complete the sentences.

The usual tip is ....   (10%   15%   20%)

Tips are ....   (included / not included in the bill)

2 Complete the conversation: ask about the meal, correct the bill, say goodbye.

WAITER : How .... the meal?

GUEST : .... May I have the ...., please?

WAITER : Here you ....

GUEST : Is service ....? Oh, ... this item correct?

WAITER : I'll just .... it again. I'm sorry, sir, it's our ....,

I'll .... that.

GUEST : Here you .... Is a credit card OK?

WAITER : Yes, that's fine. Thank you. Goodbye. We hope .... you again.

Personal job file

12 Places to visit

New words and phrases:

.... Translation ....

.... Translation ....

.... Translation ....

.... Translation ....

.... Translation ....

12.4 **1** **What are the interesting places to visit in your region?**

....

....

....

2 **Write six recommendations you make to guests. Use these expressions:**
You must visit/see /go to …   … is full of …   You shouldn't miss the …
You could go (to) …   Why not go (to) …   I'll show you on the brochure …

1 ....

2 ....

3 ....

4 ....

5 ....

6 ....

12.9 **Describe three places to visit in your region. Choose from these adjectives:**

interesting sandy modern popular busy crowded big
small exciting relaxing safe cheap expensive near far

Remember the forms:
old – older – the oldest
busy – busier – the busiest
interesting – more interesting – the most interesting

1 ....

2 ....

3 ....

Personal job file

13 Enquiries

New words and phrases:

....	Translation ....
....	Translation ....
....	Translation ....
....	Translation ....
....	Translation ....

13.4   Write a brief letter to a guest answering his/her enquiry about room rates and offer to help with any further information.

Dear ...

....

....

....

....

....

....

....

....

13.9   Write a brief letter to a guest answering his/her enquiry about conference facilities in the hotel where you work.

Dear ...

....

....

....

....

....

....

....

Personal job file

New words and phrases:

.... Translation ....

.... Translation ....

.... Translation ....

.... Translation ....

.... Translation ....

14.4 **1** How do you begin and end a telephone conversation in the hotel where you work?

Begin ....

End ....

2 A guest wants a single room with bath and balcony for three nights. Explain that you have a single room with bath, but not balcony. The guest accepts. Write a brief conversation between the hotel employee and the guest.

GUEST	I'd like a single room with bath and balcony for three nights.
EMPLOYEE	....
GUEST	....
EMPLOYEE	....
	....

14.9 Write down what an employee, answering the phone, would say in each of the following situations.

1 The caller wants to speak to a guest. The guest is not in his/her room.

....

2 The caller wants to speak to a guest whose line is busy.

....

3 The employee asks if she/he can take a message.

....

4 The employee asks if the caller wants to leave a message.

....

Personal job file

New words and phrases:

--------------------------------	Translation --------------------------------
--------------------------------	Translation --------------------------------
--------------------------------	Translation --------------------------------
--------------------------------	Translation --------------------------------
--------------------------------	Translation --------------------------------

15.4 **1** Here are four answers. Write appropriate questions.

Q: -- A: Yes, he left an hour ago.

Q: -- A: Yes, we've got everything.

Q: -- A: Yes, you're right, we have made a mistake.

Q: -- A: Yes, we've put everything on the coach.

2 Here are four questions. Write appropriate answers.

Q: How would you like to pay?   A: --------------------------------------

Q: Have you checked everything?   A: --------------------------------------

Q: Can I pay by cheque?   A: --------------------------------------

Q: Is everything ready?   A: --------------------------------------

15.9 **1** Answer these questions from the guest. Decide on the appropriate answers.

Q: Did I really make all those calls?

A: --

Q: What is this 15% charge here?

A: --

Q: I think you've made a mistake here, haven't you?

A: --

Q: Are you sure about this mini-bar amount?

A: --

2 Write down what you say to guests leaving the hotel.

Speaking practice

3.5A SPEAKING PRACTICE

Student A

Ask your partner questions in order to find all the differences
between your drawings of the same hotel room.

3.10 SPEAKING PRACTICE

Design your ideal hotel bedroom.

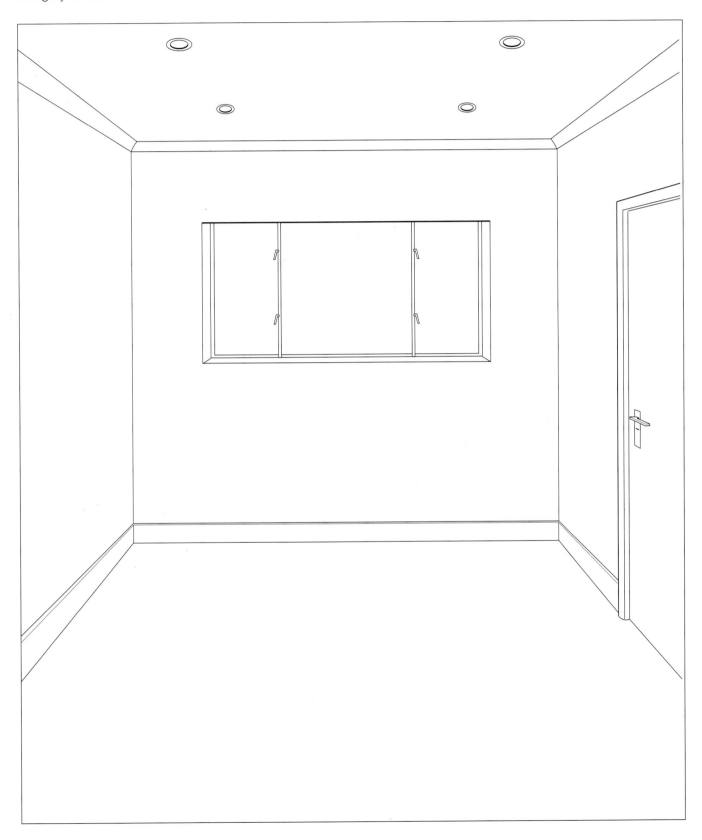

4.5 SPEAKING PRACTICE

Design your ideal hotel bathroom.

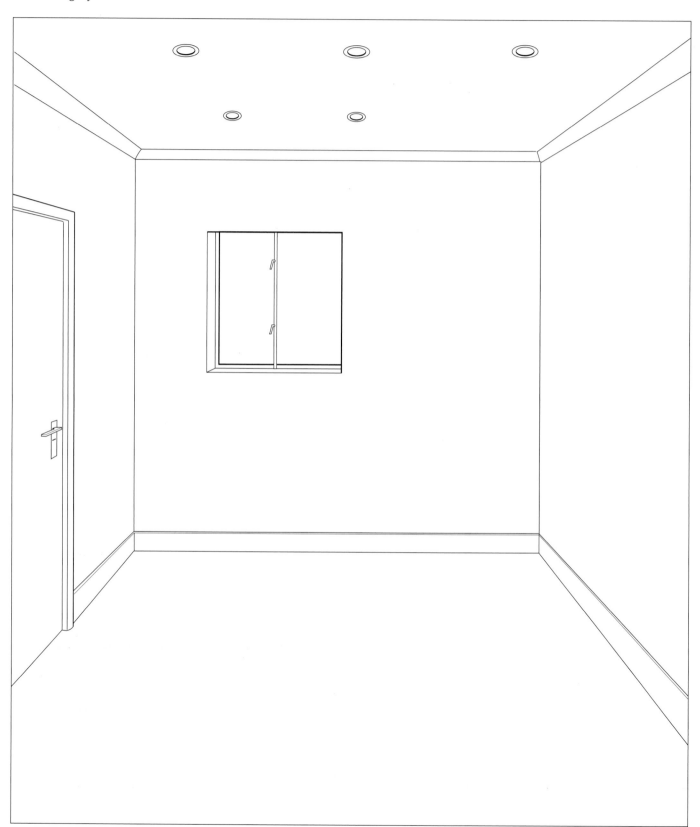

5.5A SPEAKING PRACTICE

Student A *Guest*

Ask the employee complete questions.

1

GUEST : Ask if the fitness centre is open in the evening.

EMPLOYEE : ....

2

GUEST : Ask when the bar opens.

EMPLOYEE : ....

3

GUEST : Ask if you can use the pool at any time.

EMPLOYEE : ....

4

GUEST : Ask what the check-in and check-out times are.

EMPLOYEE : ....

5

GUEST : Ask if room service is open now, at midnight.

EMPLOYEE : ....

6

GUEST : Ask if the car park is locked at night.

EMPLOYEE : ....

7

Guest : Ask if the sauna is open now, at 11 pm.

EMPLOYEE : ....

6.5A SPEAKING PRACTICE

Student A *Guest*

Ask the hotel employee for directions to the following services and write their position on the hotel plan.

business centre   gym + fitness centre
swimming pool   car park   bar   restaurant
reception   travel desk   beauty salon   gift shop

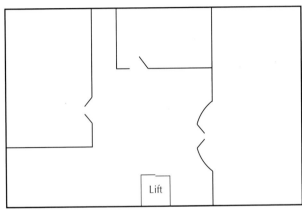

Top floor

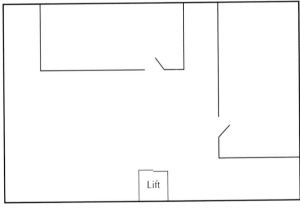

First floor

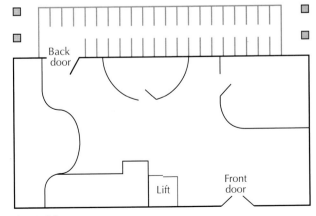

Ground floor

7.10A SPEAKING PRACTICE

Student A *Guest*

Ask for these five services at these times.

1 It is Sunday and you want the laundry service.
2 You want to use a meeting room at 7 pm on Friday.
3 You want a swim on Sunday afternoon.
4 You want to use the business centre on Saturday morning.
5 You want to leave a message for Mr Griscom.

8.5A SPEAKING PRACTICE

Student A *Guest*

Explain these problems to the hotel employee. Make complete sentences.

Problems

- No ice in mini-bar
- Sheets are dirty
- No writing paper
- No toilet paper
- Bedside light is broken
- Forgotten toothpaste
- Too much noise in next room
- No shampoo
- Want blankets not a duvet
- Want more coat hangers
- Checking out – suitcases very heavy

8.10A SPEAKING PRACTICE

Student A *Guest*

Explain the problems to the hotel employee. Make complete sentences.

Problems

- Can't find the TV channels
- Can't turn down the air-conditioning
- Can't work the electric curtains
- Can't order a film on the TV
- Can't use the bedroom safe
- Can't turn on the heating

9.5A SPEAKING PRACTICE

Student A *Guest*

Ask the bar person for suggestions and order these drinks.

- You want something very fresh, cool and non-alcoholic
- You want two drinks: brandy and sherry
- You like whisky: ask for suggestions
- Ask about the house cocktails
- You like beer: ask about draught or bottled
- You want an alcoholic drink with tonic

9.10A SPEAKING PRACTICE

Student A *Guest*

Order these drinks from the bar person.

- You'd like a double whisky and an orange juice
- You'd like a martini and a small rum
- You'd like two large draught beers
- You'd like a small brandy, a large gin and tonic, and a coke
- You'd like an orange juice, a small bottled beer, and a small whisky
- You'd like a small whisky and coke, and a small gin and tonic

10.10A SPEAKING PRACTICE

Student A *Waiter/Waitress*

∽∽ Wine list ∽∽

WINES

Red
Côtes du Rhône 1999 ... ... £19.00
Tuscany: Chianti Classico
  Riserva 1999 ... ... £21.00

Rosé
Bordeaux Château
  Thieuley 2000 ... ... £23.00

White
Soave Classico Superiore 1999 ... ... £19.50
California: Concannon £21.50

CHAMPAGNE

Krug Grande Cuvée £39.00
Roederer Brut Premier £27.00

Mineral Water: sparkling, still £3.00

French wine

Red   ***Côtes du Rhône:*** *goes with steak, seasoned meat, and pasta dishes*

Rosé ***Château Thieuley:*** *goes with light meat, and fish dishes*

Italian wine

Red   ***Chianti Classico Riserva:*** *goes with pasta, risotto, and roast meat dishes*

White ***Soave Classico Superiore:*** *goes with sea food, and light cold meat dishes*

Californian wine

White ***Concannon:*** *goes with spicy oriental dishes, pasta, fish, light meat, and vegetarian dishes*

11.10 SPEAKING PRACTICE

∽∽ Menu ∽∽

STARTERS
Smoked Salmon £8.50
Oysters £10.00
Waldorf Salad £8.50

MAIN COURSES
Rump or Fillet Steak £14.50
Roast Pork *in a Cream Sauce* £14.50
Whole Baked Trout £12.00
Sole Meunière £13.00
Steamed Turbot £12.00
Fried Prawns *with Mixed Salad* £11.00
Grilled Chicken *with Sautéed Onions* ... £12.50

DESSERTS
Fresh Fruit Salad £5.50
Apple Strudel £6.50
Trifle £7.00
Tiramisu £5.50
Chocolate soufflé £7.50
Selection of ice cream £6.00

SELECTION OF CHEESES
Brie, Gouda, Cheddar, Gruyère £4.50

COFFEE & TEA
Cappuccino, Espresso £2.00
Irish Coffee £4.00
Chinese Lotus Tea, Herbal Teas £2.00

∽∽ Wine list ∽∽

WINES

Red
Côtes du Rhône 1999 ... ... £19.00
Tuscany: Chianti Classico
  Riserva 1999 ... ... £21.00

Rosé
Bordeaux Château
  Thieuley 2000 ... ... £23.00

White
Soave Classico Superiore 1999 ... ... £19.50
California: Concannon £21.50

CHAMPAGNE

Krug Grande Cuvée £39.00
Roederer Brut Premier £27.00

Mineral Water: sparkling, still £3.00

12.5A SPEAKING PRACTICE

Student A *Guest*

You are a guest at the Carlton Hotel in New York. Study the list of interesting places to visit in New York. Ask the hotel employee for recommendations and directions.

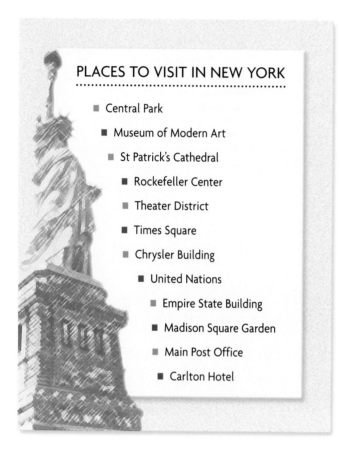

PLACES TO VISIT IN NEW YORK

- Central Park
- Museum of Modern Art
- St Patrick's Cathedral
- Rockefeller Center
- Theater District
- Times Square
- Chrysler Building
- United Nations
- Empire State Building
- Madison Square Garden
- Main Post Office
- Carlton Hotel

13.5A SPEAKING PRACTICE

Student A

Ask your partner questions in order to complete the gaps in the information about the Atlantic Hotel.

Atlantic Hotel

Room	Rate
Single	US$ ....
Double	US$ 220
Triple rooms	US$ ....
....	US$ 380
Extra bed	US$ 70

Open buffet breakfast and tax ....

Prices are subject to change without prior notice.

13.10A SPEAKING PRACTICE

Student A *Guest*

You want to enquire whether the hotel can provide these facilities for different conferences.

1 A small friendly room – to seat up to 15 people – OHPs – slides – flip charts – loudspeakers

2 A fairly large room – to seat 120 people – a full simultaneous translation service – sound equipment – VCR equipment – large screens – floral decorations

3 A large range of sound and audio-visual equipment – slides – overhead projectors – a full range of secretarial services

14.5A SPEAKING PRACTICE

Student A *Guest*

Phone and book a room at the Plaza Hotel.

1 Say hello and ask to book a room.
2 Give details of the room you'd like.
3 Say how many nights you'd like the room for.
4 Ask what is available.
5 Ask the price of a double room.
6 Accept the double room and say why you must book a room quickly.
7 Offer to confirm by e-mail.
8 Offer to send credit card details.
9 Agree with the confirmation details.
10 Say goodbye.

14.10A SPEAKING PRACTICE

Student A *Caller*

1 A Ask to speak to Jack Overton in room 782.
  B Leave this message: pick up your tickets at the airport this afternoon.

2 A Ask to speak to Holly Delroy in suite 1.
  B Leave this message: the meeting is in your suite tonight at 7.

3 A Ask to speak to Gunter Becker in room 23.
  B Leave this message: call Peter in Rome this evening, urgent.

4 A Ask to speak to Maria Marconi in room 389.
  B Leave this message: dinner booked at the Meranda restaurant at 9 pm.

15.5A SPEAKING PRACTICE

Student A *Guest*

You are checking out. Decide what you will say to the hotel employee.

GUEST	....
EMPLOYEE	Yes, Mr/Mrs Jackson, that's room 234, isn't it?
GUEST	....
EMPLOYEE	Here is your bill.
GUEST	....
EMPLOYEE	Yes, everything is included. How would you like to pay?
GUEST	....
EMPLOYEE	Yes, that's fine. Excuse me, sir/madam, I think this card has expired.

GUEST	....
EMPLOYEE	Thank you, sir/madam, could you just sign here, please?
GUEST	....
EMPLOYEE	Thank you, Mr/Mrs Jackson, and here is your receipt.
GUEST	....
EMPLOYEE	I hope you enjoyed your stay with us.

15.10A SPEAKING PRACTICE

Student A *Guest*

Discuss this bill with the hotel employee. Ask questions concerning the items marked a–f.
The notes below will help you.

a) Ask if the amount spent in the lobby lounge is correct.

b) One item was not cleaned, ask for details of prices.

c) Ask for an explanation of the service charge.

d) Ask for details of the $39 mini-bar charge.

e) Ask for details, you can't remember the call.

f) Ask for details of the transportation.

	DATE	TIME	DESCRIPTION	AMOUNT	BALANCE
a)	05/09		LOBBY LOUNGE	$37.50	$37.50
			ROOM CHARGE	$230.00	$267.50
		17.31	PRESSING	$14.00	$281.50
		17.31	DRY CLEANING	$14.00	$295.50
b)		17.32	LAUNDRY	$19.00	$314.50
c)		17.33	SERVICE CHARGE	$23.00	$337.50
	06/09		ROOM CHARGE	$230.00	$567.50
d)		12.16	MINI-BAR	$39.00	$606.50
e)		06.41	OVERSEAS CALL	$12.00	$618.50
f)		18.54	TRANSPORTATION	$25.00	$643.50

3.5B SPEAKING PRACTICE

Student B

Ask your partner questions in order to find all the differences between your drawings of the same hotel room.

5.5B SPEAKING PRACTICE

Student B *Employee*

Using this information, give complete answers to the guest's questions.

1

GUEST ....

EMPLOYEE yes – until 10.30

2

GUEST ....

EMPLOYEE opens at 4 pm

3

GUEST ....

EMPLOYEE pool open every day till 10 pm

4

GUEST ....

EMPLOYEE check-in from 2 pm; check-out by 11 am

5

GUEST ....

EMPLOYEE sorry – closes at 10.30 pm

6

GUEST ....

EMPLOYEE 24-hour valet service

7

GUEST ....

EMPLOYEE sauna closes at 10 pm, opens up tomorrow at 7 am

6.5B SPEAKING PRACTICE

Student B *Employee*

The guest has a plan of the hotel but the services are not marked on it. Answer the guest's questions about the location of these services in the hotel.

business centre   gym + fitness centre
swimming pool   car park   bar   restaurant
reception   travel desk   beauty salon   gift shop

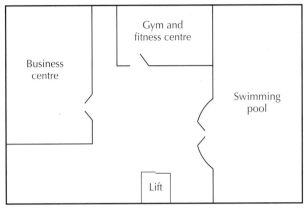

Top floor

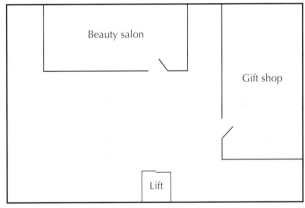

First floor

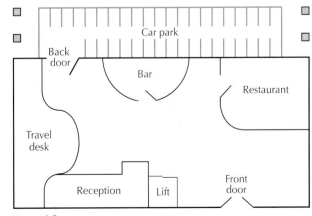

Ground floor

7.10B SPEAKING PRACTICE

Student B *Employee*

Answer the guest's questions using this information.

Laundry service:

Monday to Friday	8 am to 9 pm
Saturday	9 am to 5 pm
Sunday	Closed

Fitness centre & Swimming pool:

Monday to Friday	7 am to 10 pm
Saturday	8 am to 10 pm
Sunday	10 am to 6 pm

Business centre:

Monday to Friday	8 am to 8 pm
Saturday	10 am to 6 pm
Sunday	Closed

Meeting rooms:

Monday to Friday	7 am to 8 pm
Saturday	10 am to 6 pm
Sunday	Closed

Messages:

Mr Griscom checked out this morning.

8.5B SPEAKING PRACTICE

Student B *Employee*

Choose the best solution for each of the guest's problems. Make complete sentences.

Solutions

- Send up some more
- Inform the manager
- Contact room service
- Send maintenance up
- Get a porter for you
- Tell the housekeeper
- Bring it/them up yourself
- Contact maintenance

8.10B SPEAKING PRACTICE

Student B *Employee*

Decide what is the best solution for each of the guest's problems. Make complete sentences. Here are some words to help you:

turn on   turn off   turn up   turn down
press (the button)   tap in / key in (the code number)
choose   open   close   put in   take out

I'll show you, it works like this:

First ...

Then ...

Then ... etc.

Is that OK?

9.5B SPEAKING PRACTICE

Student B *Bar person*

Give suggestions to the guest about different drinks, and serve the drinks.

- Suggest different fresh and cool drinks
- Ask about measures, large or small; ask about sweet or dry sherry
- Suggest different types of whisky
- Describe the house cocktails
- Suggest different kinds of beer
- Ask about ice and lemon with an alcoholic drink and tonic

13.5B SPEAKING PRACTICE

Student B

Ask your partner questions in order to complete the gaps in the information about the Atlantic Hotel.

Atlantic Hotel

Room	Rate
....	US$ 140
....	US$ 220
Triple rooms	US$ 300
Suites	US$ 380
Extra bed	US$ ....

Open buffet breakfast and tax included.

Prices are subject to .... without prior notice.

12.5B SPEAKING PRACTICE

Student B *Employee*

You are an employee at the Carlton Hotel in New York. Here is part of a street plan of New York, and a list of interesting places to visit. Answer the guest's questions. Make recommendations and give directions.

14.5B SPEAKING PRACTICE

Student B *Employee*

Answer the phone and take a booking for a room.

1. Answer the phone (say 'Hello, Plaza Hotel, can I help you?').
2. Ask the caller what kind of room he/she would like.
3. Ask how many nights.
4. Check and say there are no single rooms available on these dates.
5. Say that some doubles are available.
6. Give the price of a double room.
7. Ask for confirmation by fax or e-mail.
8. Explain that you will need credit card details.
9. Confirm everything.
10. Say goodbye and that you look forward to greeting the guest when he/she arrives.

14.10B SPEAKING PRACTICE

Student B *Employee*

1. A Say that Jack Overton is not in his room. Offer to take a message.
   B Write down the message.
2. A Say that there is no reply. Offer to take a message.
   B Write down the message.
3. A Say that the line is busy. Wait, say the line is still busy, then offer to take a message.
   B Write down the message.
4. A Say that Maria Marconi is out. Offer to take a message.
   B Write down the message.

1 Central Park	7 Chrysler Building
2 Museum of Modern Art	8 United Nations
3 St Patrick's Cathedral	9 Empire State Building
4 Rockefeller Center	10 Madison Square Garden
5 Theater District	11 Main Post Office
6 Times Square	12 Carlton Hotel

15.5B SPEAKING PRACTICE

Student B *Employee*

Decide what you will say to the guest, who is checking out.

GUEST   Good morning, is my bill ready, please?

EMPLOYEE   --

GUEST   Yes, that's right.

EMPLOYEE   --

GUEST   Is everything here, including the service charge?

EMPLOYEE   --

GUEST   By credit card, is Visa OK?

EMPLOYEE   --

GUEST   Oh, yes, in that case I'll pay by American Express.

EMPLOYEE   --

GUEST   Certainly, and here is my keycard.

EMPLOYEE   --

GUEST   Thank you.

EMPLOYEE   --

15.10B SPEAKING PRACTICE

Student B *Employee*

Discuss this bill with the guest. Answer the guest's questions concerning the items marked a–f. The notes below will help you.

a) Check, say yes, give details of the drinks in the lobby lounge.

b) Check, agree it is too much, reduce the bill by $7.

c) Explain that the service charge is 10%.

d) Check, apologise, say the mini-bar charge should be $29 – reduce the bill.

e) Explain the time, destination of the call, and the charge.

f) Explain that the car hire to and from the conference centre is not free. The shuttle bus is free but not private car hire arranged by the hotel.

	DATE	TIME	DESCRIPTION	AMOUNT	BALANCE
a)	05/09		LOBBY LOUNGE	$37.50	$37.50
			ROOM CHARGE	$230.00	$267.50
		17.31	PRESSING	$14.00	$281.50
		17.31	DRY CLEANING	$14.00	$295.50
b)		17.32	LAUNDRY	$19.00	$314.50
c)		17.33	SERVICE CHARGE	$23.00	$337.50
	06/09		ROOM CHARGE	$230.00	$567.50
d)		12.16	MINI-BAR	$39.00	$606.50
e)		06.41	OVERSEAS CALL	$12.00	$618.50
f)		18.54	TRANSPORTATION	$25.00	$643.50

Tapescripts

1.2

1 Hello, I'm Zita, I'm a receptionist.
2 Hi, I'm Akoun, I'm a kitchen assistant.
3 My name's Jimmy, I'm a commissionaire.
4 Hello, I'm Shaun, I'm a sous-chef.
5 My name's Niamh, I'm a waitress.
6 Hello, my name's Taki, I'm a porter.
7 I'm Teresa, I'm a bar person.
8 Hello, my name's Anita, I'm a chambermaid.
9 I'm Yoshida, I'm a waiter.
10 Hi, my name's Kelly, I'm a management trainee.

1.2

Zita, that's Z-I-T-A.
Akoun, that's A-K-O-U-N.
Jimmy that's J-I-M-M-Y.
Shaun, that's S-H-A-U-N.
Niamh, that's N-I-A-M-H.
Taki, that's T-A-K-I.
Teresa, that's T-E-R-E-S-A.
Anita, that's A-N-I-T-A.
Yoshida, that's Y-O-S-H-I-D-A.
Kelly, that's K-E-L-L-Y.

1.7

NIAMH   Hello, my name's Niamh, I'm from Ireland.
AKOUN   Nice to meet you, Niamh. I'm Akoun.
NIAMH   Where are you from, Akoun?
AKOUN   I'm from France.
NIAMH   Oh really, which part?
AKOUN   The south, near Nice.

JIMMY   Hi, my name's Jimmy, I'm from Ireland, and you?
TAKI   Oh, hi Jimmy, my name's Taki.
JIMMY   And where are you from Taki? Greece?
TAKI   Yes, that's right.
ANITA   Good morning everyone, my name's Anita, I'm from Italy.
TERESA   Hello Anita, I'm Teresa, I'm from England and this is Yoshida, he's from Japan.
YOSHIDA Hello, pleased to meet you.

TERESA   And this is Kelly, she's from America.
KELLY   Hi everyone.

ZITA   Hi, I'm Zita.
SHAUN   Nice to meet you, I'm Shaun. Where are you from, Zita?
ZITA   I'm Irish, and you?
SHAUN   I'm from Australia.

2.2

RECEPTIONIST Hello, Globe Hotel, can I help you?
MR BOUVIER   Yes, I have a reservation from the 18th to the 21st July for a double room with bath and balcony.
RECEPTIONIST And your name please, sir?
MR BOUVIER   Bouvier.
RECEPTIONIST Could you spell that for me, please?
MR BOUVIER   Yes, that's B-O-U-V-I-E-R. I would like to change the dates, if possible, from the 19th to the 22nd July.
RECEPTIONIST Hold the line a moment and I'll just check Mr Bouvier, but I think that's possible … from the 19th to the 22nd did you say?
MR BOUVIER   Yes, that's right.
RECEPTIONIST I'm just checking … the 19th to the 22nd … Yes, that's fine Mr Bouvier, a double with bath and balcony for three nights, from the 19th to the 22nd.
MR BOUVIER   Thank you, so that's fixed up then?
RECEPTIONIST Yes, it's done, Mr Bouvier. We look forward to welcoming you on the 19th. Goodbye.
MR BOUVIER   Thank you. Goodbye.
RECEPTIONIST Goodbye.

2.7

RECEPTIONIST Good evening sir, good evening madam.
MR BOUVIER   Good evening, we have a reservation, the name's Bouvier.
RECEPTIONIST Could you spell that, please?
MR BOUVIER   B-O-U-V-I-E-R.
RECEPTIONIST Thank you. Bouvier, yes, … so that's a double room with bath and balcony for three nights.

MR BOUVIER	That's right.
RECEPTIONIST	Could you just sign here, please?
MR BOUVIER	Yes, of course.
RECEPTIONIST	Thank you sir, here's your key. It's on the fourth floor, room 401. I'll call a porter.
MR BOUVIER	Thank you.
RECEPTIONIST	Enjoy your stay.

3.2

GUEST	Can you describe the room to me, please?
EMPLOYEE	Certainly madam, let's see, first there's a big double bed, and of course there's a telephone by the bed, and you have the radio alarm next to that. Then there's a TV of course, with remote control …
GUEST	Is there a CD player in the room?
EMPLOYEE	I'm afraid there isn't a CD player in the room, madam.
GUEST	Oh well, perhaps it's not very important. But the bed sheets, are they changed every day?
EMPLOYEE	Yes, they're changed every day. And in fact the pillows are filled with a special non-allergic material. And let's see, what else? There's a large wardrobe, and there are plenty of coat hangers. Then there's a desk by the window, with two very comfortable chairs.
GUEST	Well, that seems to be just fine. OK, I'll take it.

3.7

1

GUEST	The room must be quiet.
EMPLOYEE	Of course, sir, we can give you a very quiet room on the top floor, fully equipped to the highest standards. Everything you need is included in the room. All of the rooms have full cable TV service. For your security there's a personal safe in your room and let's see … there's a trouser press next to the suitcase stand and, as a personal touch, we like to welcome our guests with a vase of flowers in the room on arrival.
GUEST	Oh, lovely.

2

EMPLOYEE	… and by each bed there's a bedside lamp and there's a central light switch as well.
GUEST	Just one thing about the bed … can I have blankets on it?

EMPLOYEE	Certainly, madam. Normally we have duvets on the bed but in some of the rooms we have ordinary blankets for guests who prefer them. So that's no problem at all.
GUEST	And will you make sure there's plenty of writing paper?
EMPLOYEE	Of course, madam.

3

EMPLOYEE	It's small but very quiet, and it does have the things you need – two big single beds and full air-conditioning.
GUEST	Is there a mini-bar in the room?
EMPLOYEE	I'm afraid there isn't a mini-bar in the room. None of the rooms have a mini-bar, but we do have a bar on the ground floor.

4

GUEST	Can you describe the room, please?
EMPLOYEE	Certainly, sir. It's a large sunny room with a view of the sea. In fact most of the rooms in the hotel do have a view of the sea. And … there's full air-conditioning of course, a mini-bar, a large desk, and there are also some nice plants in the room.

4.2

We keep extra tissues and toilet paper here in the cupboard. The shaver socket is on the wall next to the mirror. The bin is here under the washbasin. There's a hot and cold mixer tap for the shower. The bathrobe is here behind the door and the towels are on the rack over the bath. Always put plenty of soap and shampoo here, near the taps.

4.7

PORTER	Can I help you with your luggage, madam?
GUEST	Yes, please, those two red suitcases are mine.
PORTER	Shall I take the small green bag too?
GUEST	Oh yes, please bring it as well.
PORTER	This way, please, madam, the lift is just over there. […] Here you are, madam, room 233.
GUEST	Thank you, and here's something for you.
PORTER	Thank you very much, madam, I hope you enjoy your stay.

5.2

Hotel Royal Savoy, Lausanne

1

GUEST   Hello, can you tell me if the restaurant is open on Sundays, please?

EMPLOYEE   Yes, sir, it's open every evening from 7 to around 10 o'clock.

2

GUEST   Good evening, I was wondering, can I get a sauna now, I know it's a bit late?

EMPLOYEE   I'm sorry madam, the fitness and sauna closes at 10, but it opens up again tomorrow at 7 am.

3

GUEST   Can you tell me if the pool is open now?

EMPLOYEE   I'm sorry sir, the pool is only open in summer.

4

GUEST   *(on the phone from her room)* Hello, am I too late for room service?

EMPLOYEE   No, madam, room service is available until 10.30 pm.

Hotel Como, Melbourne

5

GUEST   Hello, I may be arriving a little early, what is the earliest check-in time, please?

EMPLOYEE   Normally, sir, the earliest check-in is from 2 pm and the latest check-out is at 11 am.

6

GUEST   Is the car park locked at night?

EMPLOYEE   Well, madam, it is locked, but there's 24 hour valet parking.

7

GUEST   Excuse me, what time does the bar open, please?

EMPLOYEE   At 4 pm every day, sir.

8

GUEST   I need some laundry done. Can I get these things cleaned by tonight?

EMPLOYEE   Yes, madam, there is a same-day laundry service if we have them by 11.

5.7

Hotel Grande Bretagne, Athens

EMPLOYEE   Hotel Grande Bretagne, can I help you?

GUEST   Yes, I phoned you earlier about the business facilities in your hotel, and you gave me some information. Can we just run through it again?

EMPLOYEE   Certainly, sir.

GUEST   Right, concerning secretarial services, sending faxes and so on, can you just tell me again what the hotel offers?

EMPLOYEE   Yes, indeed, well, we have a fully equipped business centre with everything you need including a full range of secretarial services, and of course up-to-date computer services with internet access, e-mail and so on. You can also send and receive faxes at any time, and we have full translation services. And if you wish we can even get you a bilingual tour guide for a trip around the city.

GUEST   Well, I'm not sure we'll get too much time for the city tour, but it sounds like a great idea. OK, let's see, that's secretarial, and we might need translations in several languages.

EMPLOYEE   That's no problem, sir. Just let us know in advance which languages you need and we can arrange everything.

GUEST   Good, well, I think that's all. I have the price list here so I'll get back to you in a day or two when I've been through it all again.

EMPLOYEE   Thank you very much, sir, we look forward to hearing from you.

Okura Garden Hotel, Shanghai

EMPLOYEE   Hello, Okura Garden Hotel, can I help you?

GUEST   Good morning, we're thinking of bringing a group for a few days to Shanghai. I'd like to know something about the amenities in your hotel, for example, can you tell me about the health and fitness centre, please?

EMPLOYEE   Of course, madam. There's a fully equipped fitness club here with an indoor swimming pool and state-of-the-art gym. You'll find all the exercise equipment you need, and there's a wonderful sauna.

GUEST   Is there a beauty salon?

EMPLOYEE   Yes, there is, madam, with our fully trained staff, of course.

GUEST   Good, so you have a full fitness centre, indoor pool, gym and a beauty salon, well, that should satisfy everybody. Now another question …

6.2

1

GUEST Can you tell me where the gift shop is, please?

EMPLOYEE Certainly, sir, the gift shop is in the basement, in fact there are several gift shops. Take the lift to the basement, and when you go out of the lift turn right, and you'll see them on your right.

GUEST Thanks.

2

GUEST Excuse me, where's the travel desk, please?

EMPLOYEE The travel desk, madam is in the main lobby, on the ground floor, right opposite the reception desk.

GUEST Sorry, I didn't catch that.

EMPLOYEE Go down to the main lobby and just opposite the reception desk you'll see the travel desk.

GUEST Oh, I see, thank you very much.

3

GUEST Excuse me, I'm looking for the bar, please.

EMPLOYEE Yes, sir, it's inside the restaurant on the ground floor. Go down to the ground floor, turn left out of the lift, and the bar is just there, on your left, inside the main restaurant.

GUEST Oh, it's inside the restaurant … I see, thanks very much.

EMPLOYEE It's a pleasure, sir.

4

GUEST Could you tell me where the fitness centre is, please?

EMPLOYEE Of course, madam, on the top floor. As you come out of the lift, it's on your left, near the swimming pool.

GUEST So that's the top floor, out of the lift, and turn left.

EMPLOYEE Yes, that's right, just next to the swimming pool.

GUEST Thank you.

EMPLOYEE You're welcome, madam.

5

GUEST Excuse me … the business centre is on the third floor, isn't it?

EMPLOYEE No, sir, it's on the second floor. Take the lift, and as you come out of the lift it's on your right, just next to the main conference rooms.

GUEST Oh, I see, on the second floor.

EMPLOYEE Yes, out of the lift, turn right, and it's next to the conference rooms.

GUEST Thank you very much.

EMPLOYEE You're welcome.

6.7

1

1

GUEST Good morning, can you help me? I'm looking for a travel agent, as I need to change my ticket.

EMPLOYEE Certainly, it's not far. Go out of the hotel and turn left. Go along Avenue de Verdun for about 100 metres and there are two travel agents on your left.

GUEST So I go out of the hotel, turn left and along Avenue de Verdun for 100 metres.

EMPLOYEE That's right.

GUEST Thank you very much.

EMPLOYEE You're welcome.

2

GUEST Can you tell me where the nearest bank is, please?

EMPLOYEE Yes, sir, it's just a few minutes walk. Go out of the hotel, turn right, go along Avenue de Verdun to Avenue de Suède, then turn right and go up Avenue de Suède until you get to Rue de la Buffa. The bank is on the corner, on your right.

GUEST So that's out of the hotel, right, right again up to Rue de la Buffa.

EMPLOYEE Yes, and the bank's on the corner.

GUEST Thanks very much.

EMPLOYEE It's a pleasure.

3

GUEST I'm looking for a photo shop, please.

EMPLOYEE There's one very near the hotel in Avenue de Suède. Go out of the hotel, turn right and go along to Avenue de Suède. Turn right into Avenue de Suède, and you'll see the photo shop opposite.

GUEST Avenue de Suède, OK, thank you.

EMPLOYEE You're welcome.

4

GUEST Is the cinema far from here, please?

EMPLOYEE It's about a 10-minute walk from here, sir. Turn left out of the hotel, and go along Avenue de Verdun until you get to Avenue Jean Médecin. Turn left, go up Avenue Jean Médecin, and there are two cinemas, one on your left and one on your right.

GUEST Let me see, that's left along Avenue de Verdun until I get to Avenue Jean Médecin.

EMPLOYEE That's right. Here, I can show you on the map.

GUEST Thank you.

EMPLOYEE You're welcome.

5

GUEST Is there a cash point near here, please?

EMPLOYEE Yes, it's not far. Go out of the hotel, turn right, then right again into Avenue de Suède. Go up the street to the corner, and there on the corner, on your right, is the cash point next to the bank.

GUEST So that's out of the hotel, turn right, and right again into Avenue de Suède, and then up that street to the corner.

EMPLOYEE That's it, madam, the cash point is on the corner, on your right next to the bank.

GUEST Next to the bank, yes, of course. Thank you.

EMPLOYEE You're welcome.

6.7

EMPLOYEE It's not very far, about 15 minutes on foot, five minutes by car. Go out of the hotel into Avenue de Verdun. Turn left and go along Avenue de Verdun until you get to Place Masséna. Turn left at Place Masséna into Avenue Jean Médecin. Go along Avenue Jean Médecin until you get to Avenue Thiers – it's about 500 metres. Turn left and it's just there on your right.

7.2

1

Guest 1

ROOM SERVICE Hello, room service, can I help you?

GUEST Yes, I want to order a meal … let's see, the caesar salad to start with, with bruschetta and then some fish. I see there's cod and salmon …

ROOM SERVICE Yes, both are very good, fresh today, of course.

GUEST OK, well, I think I'll go for the salmon.

ROOM SERVICE That's the sesame salmon, isn't it? There's also the smoked salmon.

GUEST Yes, yes, not the smoked salmon, and I'd like some ice cream. Oh, no, wait a moment, how about the apple strudel, that comes with ice cream, doesn't it?

ROOM SERVICE Yes, madam, vanilla ice cream.

GUEST Good, I'll have that then.

ROOM SERVICE So, that's the caesar salad, bruschetta, the sesame salmon, and the apple strudel. Would you like anything else, madam?

GUEST That's it, thank you.

ROOM SERVICE And your room number, please.

GUEST Oh, 391.

Guest 2

ROOM SERVICE Hello, room service, can I help you?

GUEST Can you bring up a couple of meals as soon as possible, please? Is everything on the menu available?

ROOM SERVICE Yes, sir.

GUEST OK, then the grilled goat's cheese to start with. And put the baguette with that. That's with brie, isn't it?

ROOM SERVICE Yes, sir, chicken, bacon and brie baguette.

GUEST Good, and a mixed salad.

ROOM SERVICE Is that just one mixed salad?

GUEST Yes, just one, then the steak, well done please, the penne pasta, and the crème brûlée. No, wait, make that the chicken instead of the steak.

ROOM SERVICE Right, sir, so that's the goat's cheese, mixed salad, and the chicken, not the steak, isn't it?

GUEST Yes, the chicken.

ROOM SERVICE … then the penne pasta and the crème brûlée.

GUEST That's it, and don't forget the baguette.

ROOM SERVICE … plus the baguette. That will be ready in about 15 minutes.

GUEST And it's for two people, in suite 21.

ROOM SERVICE Right, sir, for two people … suite 21. Thank you.

7.2

2

Guest 1

GUEST Look, this isn't right. I ordered the cajun salmon, not the smoked salmon, and I definitely asked for a caesar salad, not this green salad. Oh dear, and you've brought the ice cream when I'm sure I said the cheese board.

WAITER I'm very sorry, madam, there's been a mistake, I'll change this immediately.

Guest 2

GUEST I'm afraid there's been a mistake. Are you sure you didn't mix me up with somebody else? I ordered the mixed green salad, not the caesar salad, the garlic bread, not the bruschetta, and tiramisu and you've brought the crème brûlée.

WAITER Oh, I'm extremely sorry, sir, I'll correct this at once.

7.7

1

HOUSEKEEPER Housekeeping department, can I help you?

GUEST Yes, I need my suit pressed, but I'm in a hurry. I know it's late but can you get it done this evening?

HOUSEKEEPER I'm sorry, sir, but today is Saturday, and the laundry service closed at 5 pm.

GUEST Oh, how annoying.

2

RECEPTION Good afternoon, madam, can I help you?

GUEST Yes, I'd like some information about the pool. Is it open on Sundays?

RECEPTION Yes, it's open now but I'm afraid it closes at 6 pm.

GUEST I see, thank you.

3

GUEST Hello, is that reception?

EMPLOYEE Yes, can I help you?

GUEST Yes, we're in a meeting now which will go on till 9 o'clock or even later. Is that OK for the room?

EMPLOYEE Well, normally the meeting rooms close at 8 pm Monday to Friday.

GUEST Ah! So we can't go on after 8 o'clock, is that right?

EMPLOYEE That's right, sir, I'm afraid it's not possible to keep the rooms open after 8 pm; you see all the staff go off duty.

GUEST Of course, yes.

4

GUEST Can I get into the fitness centre now? I know it's a bit early.

EMPLOYEE Well, it's not open just yet, madam; it doesn't open until 8 am.

GUEST OK, I'll wait until 8. Thank you.

EMPLOYEE You're welcome.

5

GUEST Hello, I'd like to leave a message for Mrs Jones in room 620, please.

RECEPTION Mrs Jones … I'll just have a look … I'm afraid Mrs Jones checked out this morning at 8.30.

GUEST Oh, she's checked out already. I see, well I'll contact her office then, thank you.

RECEPTION You're welcome.

8.2

1

GUEST Hello, reception, this is room 329. We've managed to empty the mini-bar. Could you get someone to restock it, please?

RECEPTION Certainly, madam. Is there anything in particular you need?

GUEST Yes, well, a bit of everything really, especially plenty of whisky and coke.

RECEPTION I'll send someone up right away.

GUEST Thank you.

2

GUEST Hello, reception, I'm afraid I've forgotten my hair dryer. I wonder if you could send one up to my room?

RECEPTION Well, madam, there should be one in your room. Have you had a look in the bathroom, by the basin?

GUEST Yes, and I can't see one.

RECEPTION I'm sorry about that. I'll see to it immediately. And your room number, please?

GUEST Room 309.

3

GUEST Look I've just arrived in the room, and I don't know what's happened, but the sheets are dirty. Can you change them, please?

RECEPTION Oh, I'm very sorry, that shouldn't happen. What room are you in?

GUEST 709.

RECEPTION I'll contact housekeeping now.

4

GUEST Hello, is that reception?

RECEPTION Speaking.

GUEST My wife and I have rather a lot of clothes and we need some more coat hangers. We're in room 438.

RECEPTION I'll get someone to bring some up at once.

5

GUEST Oh, hello, is that reception? Look, I've forgotten all my shaving stuff. Can I get a razor and some shaving cream, please?

RECEPTION Yes, we can provide all these items. If you would like to contact housekeeping they will be able to help you. Just dial 121.

GUEST Oh, 121, I see … thank you.

8.7

The TV

RECEPTION Hello, can I help you?

GUEST Yes, I'm having a bit of trouble with the TV.

RECEPTION Oh, is it not working?

GUEST No, no, it seems to be working all right, but I want to get a film, and it just keeps going fuzzy.

RECEPTION OK, have you got the remote control?

GUEST Yes.

RECEPTION Right … you want to order a film?

GUEST Yes, that's right.

RECEPTION OK, perhaps it's best if you switch off everything first – that's the green button on the left of the screen.

GUEST OK, everything's off.

RECEPTION Now switch on the TV – that's the same green button.

GUEST OK.

RECEPTION Then press Video on the remote control.

GUEST Video, OK, done.

RECEPTION You will see a list of films.

GUEST Ah, yes, on the top here …

RECEPTION Select a film, use the arrows on the remote control to go up or down, then press OK.

GUEST Oh, I see, you have to press OK.

RECEPTION That's right, then when you press Play the film begins …

GUEST I see, it's simple really, but I'm not very good with these machines.

RECEPTION Don't worry, it's the same for many people. Is that OK now?

GUEST Yes, thank you very much.

RECEPTION You're welcome, enjoy the film.

The safe

GUEST Is that reception?

RECEPTION Yes, reception, can I help you?

GUEST Yes, please. It's the safe in the room.

RECEPTION Is there something wrong?

GUEST Well, it's just that I want to put some jewellery in it, but I'm not sure how it works. There's no key …

RECEPTION No, madam, it works on a code system. You can choose your own code number for the safe. But there should be a little card explaining how it works by the safe.

GUEST Oh, I can't see one.

RECEPTION Well, I'm sorry about that. I'll send one up, but do you want to lock some valuables away now?

GUEST Yes, please.

RECEPTION So, OK, open the safe door, put your valuables in and close the door. On the front of the door you will see some letters and numbers.

GUEST Letters and numbers? Oh, yes, I see.

RECEPTION Now tap A, then tap a six digit number, then tap C. Remember this number, you'll need it to open the door again.

GUEST What's that again?

RECEPTION	Tap A, then tap a six digit number, then tap C and remember this number, because you'll need it to open the door again.
GUEST	So I tap A, then six numbers, then C – so I choose any six numbers?
RECEPTION	That's right, and when you've done that, turn the dial quickly and the safe is locked.
GUEST	So, that's A then six numbers, then C, then turn the dial quickly.
RECEPTION	That's right madam. So, to open the door again, tap A then your code number, turn the dial and the door will open.
GUEST	Tap A, the code, turn the dial … OK, I see, but supposing I can't open it again?
RECEPTION	Don't worry, if you really get stuck I'll send someone up to help you.
GUEST	Oh, thank you, well, I'll have a go then.
RECEPTION	You're welcome.

9.2

1

BAR PERSON	Good afternoon, madam, what can I get you?
GUEST	Just a dry martini, please.
BAR PERSON	Right, madam. A dry martini.

2

BAR PERSON	Good evening, madam, what would you like to drink?
GUEST	Two glasses of white wine, please, and a small orange juice.
BAR PERSON	Certainly, madam.

3

BAR PERSON	Good evening, sir, what can I get you?
GUEST	Let's see, a small beer, a small vodka and orange, and a coke, please.
BAR PERSON	Small beer, vodka and orange, and a coke. Would you like ice and lemon in the vodka?
GUEST	Just some ice, please.

4

BAR PERSON	We have a wonderful local beer …
GUEST	Is it draught or bottled?
BAR PERSON	Both, sir, we have large and small bottles, and we have it on draught too.
GUEST	OK, I'll try that, but not draught; a large bottled beer then, and a small glass of rum.

5

BAR PERSON	I'm sorry, madam, we don't have that type of mineral water, but we do have this one; it's very good.
GUEST	That's fine then, half a bottle, please.
BAR PERSON	Here you are, madam.

6

BAR PERSON	This house cocktail is excellent, sir.
GUEST	OK, then make that two, and a large gin and tonic.
BAR PARSON	Here you are, sir.

9.7

1

BAR PERSON	Here you are, madam, a small rum and a dry martini. Shall I charge it to your room?
GUEST	No, I'll pay cash. How much is that?
BAR PERSON	That comes to €11.50.
GUEST	Thanks, here, keep the change.
BAR PERSON	Thank you, madam.

2

BAR PERSON	Here you are, sir, two large draught beers, a whisky, and a vodka. And are you staying in the hotel?
GUEST	No, I'm not. How much does that come to?
BAR PERSON	That's €23.50, sir.
GUEST	I'll pay by Visa, here you are.
BAR PERSON	Thank you, sir.

3

BAR PERSON	What can I get you, madam?
GUEST	I'd like a gin and tonic, and a coke with plenty of ice.
BAR PERSON	Lemon with the gin, madam?
GUEST	Yes, please and, oh, wait a moment … and a small draught beer, please.
BAR PERSON	Right, a gin and tonic, a coke and a small draught beer … Here you are. Shall I charge it to your room?
GUEST	Yes, please.
BAR PERSON	That's €13, madam. Could you sign here, please?

4

BAR PERSON	Here you are, sir, a double brandy, a rum and coke, and a tonic water. That comes to €24.
GUEST	Look, I'll pay by cheque … here you are.
BAR PERSON	Thank you, sir.

10.2

1

WAITRESS	Here is the menu.
GUESTS	Thank you.
WAITRESS	Can I get you something to drink? Would you like an aperitif?
MALE GUEST	How about you?
FEMALE GUEST	Yes, please … now let's see …

2

MALE GUEST	Could I have another martini, please?
WAITRESS	Certainly, I'll bring it at once.

3

WAITRESS	Good evening, sir, good evening, madam.
GUESTS	Good evening.
WAITRESS	Do you have a reservation?
MALE GUEST	Yes, a table for two …
WAITRESS	And your name, please?
MALE GUEST	The name's Griscom.

4

WAITRESS	Good evening, madam. Have you got a reservation?
FEMALE GUEST	No, we don't have a reservation I'm afraid.
WAITRESS	In that case, I'm sorry, we're fully booked tonight.

5

WAITRESS	Shall I take your coat, madam?
FEMALE GUEST	Yes, thank you.

10.7

WAITRESS	Are you ready to order, madam?
FEMALE GUEST	Yes, I think so. Just a question, what is the waldorf salad?
WAITRESS	It's a crispy salad with cheese and croutons.
MALE GUEST	It's not a mixed salad?
WAITRESS	No, it's fresh lettuce with dressing and the cheese and croutons mixed in.
FEMALE GUEST	OK, I'll have that.
WAITRESS	… and something to follow?
FEMALE GUEST	I'd like some fish, please. Can you recommend something?
WAITRESS	The sole meunière is very good, madam, and very popular.
FEMALE GUEST	Is it fresh today?
WAITRESS	Absolutely.

FEMALE GUEST	Fine, I'll have that then.
WAITRESS	Thank you, and you, sir?
MALE GUEST	Just a steak for me, please, no starter.
WAITRESS	How would you like it – rare, medium or well done?
MALE GUEST	Well done, please.
WAITRESS	And what would you like to drink?
MALE GUEST	How about a bottle of rosé?
FEMALE GUEST	And a bottle of sparkling mineral water, please.
WAITRESS	So that's the waldorf salad and the sole meunière, steak, well done, a bottle of rosé and a bottle of sparkling mineral water. Thank you.

11.2

WAITRESS	Would you like to see the cheese tray?
MAN	Yes, why not?
WOMAN	Nothing for me, thanks.
MAN	Let's see, I'd like a little brie and some cheddar, please.
WAITRESS	Certainly, sir, and can I take your order for dessert?
WOMAN	I fancy some chocolate. I think I saw something on the menu …
WAITRESS	Yes, indeed, madam, if you like chocolate, I can recommend the chocolate soufflé.
WOMAN	Sounds perfect. I'll go for it.
MAN	The trifle sounds pretty good, and the apple strudel too.
WAITRESS	Yes, they're both very good – the trifle is made with sherry, and the apple strudel is very traditional of course, served hot with ice cream.
MAN	That's for me then. I'll have the apple strudel.
WAITRESS	So that's the chocolate soufflé and the strudel. And some coffee or tea?
WOMAN	A cappuccino for me, please.
MAN	An espresso, please.
WAITRESS	Thank you, so that's an espresso and a cappuccino. Thank you.

11.7

WAITRESS Was everything all right, sir?

MAN Yes, thank you, just fine.

WOMAN The chocolate soufflé was delicious …

WAITRESS Thank you, madam. Is there anything else I can get you?

MAN No, I don't think so …

WOMAN Not for me …

MAN Can I have the bill, please? Oh, and can I pay by Visa?

WAITRESS That's no problem, sir, we accept all types of credit cards. […] Here you are, sir.

MAN Thank you. Excuse me, but is this item correct?

WAITRESS Which one, sir?

MAN Here, I thought we had only one bottle of wine and a mineral water.

WAITRESS Oh, I'm very sorry, sir, I'll check that for you. […] Here you are, we've corrected the mistake.

MAN OK, is service included?

WAITRESS Yes, sir, it's included.

MAN Here's my credit card.

WAITRESS Thank you. […] Goodnight and thank you.

MAN AND WOMAN Goodnight.

WAITRESS We hope to see you again.

12.2

Guest 1

GUEST Hello, can you help me? We've a few hours free this afternoon, and we'd like to see some of the sights. What do you suggest we visit?

EMPLOYEE Well, sir, New York is full of great places to visit – museums, art galleries, concerts, famous buildings … do you have any particular interest?

GUEST Well, yes, art. We'd like to visit some of the famous art galleries. And we'd like to do some shopping.

EMPLOYEE You've come to the right place, sir. The Museum of Modern Art is only a few minutes from here. You must see it while you're here. And the shopping district of 5th Avenue is very close too. Here, I'll show you on the map.

GUEST Thank you.

EMPLOYEE You're welcome.

Guest 2

GUEST My husband and I would like to visit the city. Can you recommend some places to go?

EMPLOYEE Certainly, madam, New York is full of very interesting places to go to. I'll show you a few here on the brochure. Here's the Statue of Liberty – you'd like the trip there. And you shouldn't miss the Empire State Building – the view from the top is one of the best in New York. Or here, look, you could go down to the theatre district on Broadway – there are some great shows there at the moment. Or of course you could go shopping on 5th Avenue … here you can see it on the map.

GUEST Is the Empire State Building open every day?

EMPLOYEE Oh, yes, every day from 9.30 am to midnight. And it's not very far from here.

GUEST Sounds great, thanks.

EMPLOYEE You're welcome.

Guest 3

GUEST Could you tell me where I'll find a really good tour of the city?

EMPLOYEE Yes, madam, there are a few here to choose from. Look, I'll show you the brochure …

GUEST And what about music? I like all kinds of music.

EMPLOYEE You're in luck. There's a free concert today in Central Park . Why not go to it? I'll just get you the information … here's a brochure for you, and here's a list of all the other concerts in the city at the moment.

GUEST Thank you very much.

EMPLOYEE You're welcome.

13.2

Guest 1

GUEST Hello, is that the Stars Hotel?

EMPLOYEE Yes, madam, can I help you?

GUEST I'm enquiring about the room rates at your hotel. Could you tell me, please, how much a double room is?

EMPLOYEE Yes, of course. Well, double rooms or twin rooms are from $240 to 280 a night.

GUEST And you have a number of executive suites too?

EMPLOYEE Yes, we do. The suites range from $550 to 1,000 per night.

GUEST Is there a service charge included in the price?

EMPLOYEE No, madam, the service charge is 15%.

GUEST I see, OK, so that's doubles $280 …

EMPLOYEE $280 is the top price. The doubles are from $240 to 280 a night.

GUEST Yes, thanks, and the suites $550 to 1,000.

EMPLOYEE That's right, and the service charge is 15%.

GUEST I think I have all that. Thank you very much.

EMPLOYEE You're welcome.

Guest 2

GUEST Hello, is that the Devonshire Arms?

EMPLOYEE Yes, good evening, can I help you, madam?

GUEST I'm telephoning to get some information on room rates. What's the price of a single room, please?

EMPLOYEE The basic single rooms are £75. But we do have a superior twin single room for £95.

GUEST I see, and the suites, how much are they, please?

EMPLOYEE The suites are £200 per night.

GUEST And does this include breakfast?

EMPLOYEE Yes, madam, the price includes a full English breakfast and of course the price also includes VAT.

GUEST I see, so I'll just check that, singles £75 and £95 with a full English breakfast.

EMPLOYEE That's right.

GUEST And what did you say about VAT?

EMPLOYEE VAT is included in the price.

GUEST Yes, of course. I see, thank you very much. I think I've got that – singles at 75 and 95 and suites at 200, with breakfast and VAT included.

EMPLOYEE That's right, madam.

GUEST Thank you very much.

EMPLOYEE It's a pleasure.

Guest 3

GUEST Hello, is that the Il Capello Hotel?

EMPLOYEE Speaking, how can I help you?

GUEST I'm just checking the room rates. I have a price list from last year but I expect the prices have changed. How much are the single rooms this year, please?

EMPLOYEE Well, sir, the rates have changed slightly since last year. The singles are now from €180 to €240.

GUEST And the doubles?

EMPLOYEE The twin or double rooms are now €270 to €330.

GUEST That includes tax and service charge I imagine?

EMPLOYEE Yes, the tax and the service charge are included, but the price doesn't include breakfast, which is €18.

GUEST Thank you very much. I think I've got that … that's singles now at 180 to 240, doubles to 270.

EMPLOYEE No, the price of doubles is from €270 to €330.

GUEST Oh, I see, that's doubles from 270 to 330 and breakfast is €18. Oh, and can I get an extra bed if we need one?

EMPLOYEE Yes, of course, an extra bed is €45.

GUEST €45. OK, that's fine. Thank you very much.

EMPLOYEE You're welcome.

13.7

Guest 1

GUEST Hello, can you help me? I'm enquiring about the conference facilities at your hotel. I believe you have a range of services. I'm particularly looking for a small friendly room, say, to seat up to 50 or 60 people, to hold a series of meetings.

EMPLOYEE Certainly, madam, we can do that for you. Our meeting rooms have a very relaxed atmosphere and we can seat up to 80 people.

GUEST Can I perhaps just run through the things we need?

EMPLOYEE Sure, go ahead.

GUEST OK, we're going to need all the usual audio-visual equipment, particularly overhead projectors, slides, flip charts. And we're also looking for VCR equipment.

EMPLOYEE All that's no problem, madam, we have all the latest audio-visual equipment, including of course VCRs.

GUEST Good. Another thing – can you provide simultaneous translation?

EMPLOYEE Yes, madam, we have a full team of translators that we employ. If you would like to specify which languages, we would be happy to accommodate.

GUEST Sure, I can do that. So that's room, equipment, translators all seem to be OK.

EMPLOYEE Do you have our conference pack which gives full details of all the conference facilities?

GUEST No, in fact.

EMPLOYEE We'll send you one, if you let me have an address.

GUEST Sure and then I'll get back to you with all these details. My address is …

Guest 2

GUEST Good morning. My name's Mr Thompson, I phoned you a few days ago for information about your conference facilities, and you kindly sent me your conference pack.

EMPLOYEE Yes, hello, Mr Thompson.

GUEST Can I just clarify a few points?

EMPLOYEE Certainly, sir.

GUEST I believe you have a large range of audio-visual equipment.

EMPLOYEE Yes, indeed, we can supply all the latest audio-visual equipment.

GUEST Actually, we will need some large screens for computer projection, and of course loudspeakers.

EMPLOYEE Yes, sir, again that's no problem. If it's not actually in the hotel we can certainly arrange to get it.

GUEST Good – something else. Can you do a nice floral decoration, nothing too elaborate, just something simple to add a bit of colour?

EMPLOYEE Yes, if you'd like to specify what you'd like, we have several different arrangements we can offer.

GUEST Well, look, perhaps the best thing is that I e-mail all this to you and we can take it from there.

EMPLOYEE Do you have our e-mail address?

GUEST Yes, I do, thank you.

EMPLOYEE Good, we look forward to hearing from you.

14.2

EMPLOYEE Good morning, Plaza Hotel, can I help you?

GUEST Yes, I phoned last week about a room but I didn't book anything. Can I make a reservation now?

EMPLOYEE Certainly, madam, what kind of room would you like?

GUEST Well, do you still have a single room with bath from the 19th March?

EMPLOYEE For how many nights, madam?

GUEST Three nights, from the 19th to the 22nd March.

EMPLOYEE I'll just check, but I think all the singles have gone for that weekend. … I'm very sorry, madam, but we have no more singles for that weekend.

GUEST Oh dear, that's a pity. I should have booked last week. Do you have any doubles left?

EMPLOYEE Let me see, yes, madam, there's just one double left.

GUEST And how much is it?

EMPLOYEE It's $130 per night, not including breakfast.

GUEST I see, and the single is $95.

EMPLOYEE That's right.

GUEST Are you sure that's all that's left for that weekend?

EMPLOYEE I'm afraid so, there's quite a demand, especially for singles, with the conference here that weekend.

GUEST Yes, of course. I'm going to that conference too. OK, I'd better take the double then.

EMPLOYEE Right, madam, and your name, please?

GUEST It's Mrs Delaporte, that's D-E-L-A-P-O-R-T-E.

EMPLOYEE Could you please confirm that by fax or e-mail, Mrs Delaporte, and we'll need a credit card number and expiry date, please.

GUEST Of course.

EMPLOYEE So that's a double room with bath from the 19th to the 22nd March. We'll hold the room until 6 pm. We look forward to seeing you on the 19th.

GUEST Thank you, goodbye.

14.7

1

EMPLOYEE Hello, Plaza Hotel, can I help you?

CALLER Yes, can you put me through to Mr Jackson, it's room 132.

EMPLOYEE … I'm afraid the line is busy, would you like to hold?

CALLER OK, I'll hold.

EMPLOYEE … The line's still busy, I'm afraid.

CALLER I'll leave a message: will you tell Mr Jackson to call Peter at home?

EMPLOYEE Certainly, sir.

2

EMPLOYEE Hello, Plaza Hotel, can I help you?

CALLER Yes, good morning, room number 529, please, Angela Morris should be there.

EMPLOYEE I'll put you through. … I'm afraid there's no answer, can I take a message?

CALLER Yes, it's Mr Mori – that's M-O-R-I. I'll call again later.

3

EMPLOYEE Good morning, Plaza Hotel, can I help you?

CALLER Yes, good morning, can I speak to Bill Preston in suite 2?

EMPLOYEE Right, madam, just connecting you. … I'm afraid there's no answer, would you like to leave a message?

CALLER Oh dear, yes, tell him I'll meet him in the hotel bar at 7 pm.

EMPLOYEE And your name, please?

CALLER It's Paola Neri.

EMPLOYEE Could you spell that, please?

CALLER Yes, it's P-A-O-L-A N-E-R-I.

EMPLOYEE Thank you, I'll make sure he gets the message.

CALLER Thank you.

4

EMPLOYEE The Plaza Hotel, can I help you?

CALLER Yes, I'd like to speak to Jacqueline Dupont, in room number 398, please.

EMPLOYEE I think I saw her leave, I'll just check. … I'm sorry, madam, but there's no reply from her room.

CALLER Can I leave a message?

EMPLOYEE Yes, of course.

CALLER Tell her to call the office as soon as possible, would you?

EMPLOYEE Certainly, I'll make sure she gets the message.

CALLER Thank you.

15.2

1

EMPLOYEE Good morning, sir.

GUEST Good morning, I'd like to check out, please, it's Mr Lopez, 239. Is my bill ready?

EMPLOYEE Yes, Mr Lopez, here you are.

GUEST Let's see, €473. Is service included?

EMPLOYEE Yes, sir, it is.

GUEST OK, that looks fine. Can I pay by credit card?

EMPLOYEE Yes, of course, sir.

GUEST Is MasterCard OK?

EMPLOYEE Of course, sir.

2

EMPLOYEE Can I help you, madam?

GUEST Yes, I'd like to settle my bill now, room 359 … the name's Kim Sung. I don't have my credit cards, I'll pay cash.

EMPLOYEE Here it is, madam. It comes to €390.

GUEST Ah, I don't think I have that much. I'd better pay by cheque.

EMPLOYEE We'll need some identification.

GUEST Oh, yes, is my passport all right?

EMPLOYEE That's fine.

GUEST Here you are.

EMPLOYEE Thank you. Would you just sign here, please?

3

EMPLOYEE Here's a copy of your bill, sir, and we've charged it to your company as you requested.

GUEST Thank you. How much does it come to?

EMPLOYEE Here you are, it's €983.

GUEST Is everything included, the dinners, the meeting rooms we used and so on?

EMPLOYEE Everything's here, sir.

GUEST Good. Do I just sign here?

EMPLOYEE Yes, please, on the bottom of the form, here.

GUEST OK.

EMPLOYEE And here is your receipt.

4

GUEST Is my bill ready, please?

EMPLOYEE Yes, madam, here it is. How would you like to settle your account?

GUEST I'll pay cash. Let's see – how much is it?

EMPLOYEE This is the total, madam, €223.

GUEST And can I leave a tip for the staff?

EMPLOYEE That's very kind of you.

GUEST Here you are, one hundred, two hundred and fifty … that covers the bill, and something for the staff.

EMPLOYEE Thank you very much. Here's your receipt.

GUEST Thank you.

15.7

EMPLOYEE Good morning, madam, can I help you?

GUEST Yes, could you explain these items on my bill, please?

EMPLOYEE Certainly, madam, what would you like to know?

GUEST Well, why are there two charges for dry cleaning and laundry?

EMPLOYEE Yes, that's the usual practice, the laundry is charged separately.

GUEST Oh, I see. And did I really make three phone calls overseas? I thought it was only two.

EMPLOYEE I'll check again … yes, our records show you made three calls overseas … here are the times and dates …

GUEST Oh, did I really? I'd forgotten. And this is the room charge of course. But what's this 10% charge here, please?

EMPLOYEE That's the 10% service charge in lieu of gratuities.

GUEST Ah I see … and I can't quite make out this part …

EMPLOYEE Oh sorry, it seems to be badly printed out … these two items are the mini-bar we restocked, and car you ordered last week.

GUEST The mini-bar OK, but the car?

EMPLOYEE Yes, that's for the car you ordered last week to go to the conference centre. The shuttle bus is free but not transportation by car.

GUEST Oh, I didn't realise that, cars and shuttle buses were advertised.

EMPLOYEE Yes, but a private car was extra.

GUEST Well, yes, I guess so.

EMPLOYEE Is everything OK now, madam?

GUEST Yes, I think so.

EMPLOYEE And here's your receipt. I hope you enjoyed your stay with us.

GUEST Yes, thank you.

EMPLOYEE Have a good day, madam, and we hope to see you again.

Verb list

Write the translation of each verb.

Translation	Infinitive	Past simple	Past participle
....	ask	asked	asked
....	be	was	been
....	book	booked	booked
....	call	called	called
....	charge	charged	charged
....	check	checked	checked
....	choose	chose	chosen
....	close	closed	closed
....	come	came	come
....	confirm	confirmed	confirmed
....	connect	connected	connected
....	contact	contacted	contacted
....	correct	corrected	corrected
....	deal	dealt	dealt
....	do	did	done
....	enjoy	enjoyed	enjoyed
....	expire	expired	expired
....	find	found	found
....	finish	finished	finished
....	follow	followed	followed
....	get	got	got
....	give	gave	given
....	go	went	gone
....	have	had	had
....	hesitate	hesitated	hesitated
....	hold	held	held
....	hope	hoped	hoped
....	include	included	included
....	leave	left	left
....	like	liked	liked
....	look	looked	looked

Verb list

Translation	Infinitive	Past simple	Past participle
----------------------------	make	made	made
----------------------------	meet	met	met
----------------------------	miss	missed	missed
----------------------------	need	needed	needed
----------------------------	notice	noticed	noticed
----------------------------	open	opened	opened
----------------------------	order	ordered	ordered
----------------------------	pay	paid	paid
----------------------------	phone	phoned	phoned
----------------------------	prefer	preferred	preferred
----------------------------	press	pressed	pressed
----------------------------	put	put	put
----------------------------	recommend	recommended	recommended
----------------------------	reserve	reserved	reserved
----------------------------	say	said	said
----------------------------	seat	seated	seated
----------------------------	see	saw	seen
----------------------------	send	sent	sent
----------------------------	settle	settled	settled
----------------------------	show	showed	shown
----------------------------	sign	signed	signed
----------------------------	sit	sat	sat
----------------------------	stay	stayed	stayed
----------------------------	suggest	suggested	suggested
----------------------------	take	took	taken
----------------------------	tell	told	told
----------------------------	thank	thanked	thanked
----------------------------	think	thought	thought
----------------------------	try	tried	tried
----------------------------	turn	turned	turned
----------------------------	visit	visited	visited
----------------------------	welcome	welcomed	welcomed